FIRST
FIELD
GUIDE

SHELLS

NATIONAL AUDUBON SOCIETY®

FIRST FIELD GUIDE

SHELLS

Written by
Brian Cassie

Scholastic Inc.

New York   Toronto   London   Auckland   Sydney
Mexico City   New Delhi   Hong Kong

The National Audubon Society, established in 1905, has 550,000 members and more than 500 chapters nationwide. Its mission is to conserve and restore natural ecosystems, focusing on wildlife and plant life, and these guides are part of that mission. Celebrating the beauty and wonders of nature, Audubon is embarking upon its second century of educating people of all ages. For information about Audubon membership, contact:

National Audubon Society
700 Broadway
New York, NY 10003-9562
800-274-4201
http://www.audubon.org/

LIBRARY OF CONGRESS CATALOGING-IN-PUBLICATION DATA

Cassie, Brian, 1953–
    National Audubon Society first field guide. Shells / written
by Brian Cassie.
        p.   cm.
    Summary: Provides information about mollusks and their shells
and how to identify them, along with detailed descriptions and
photographs of fifty common North American shells.
    ISBN 0-590-64233-2 (hc.) — ISBN 0-590-64258-8 (pb.)
    1. Shells—Identification—Juvenile literature. 2. Mollusks—
Juvenile literature. [1. Shells—Identification. 2. Mollusks] I. Title:
Shells. II. National Audubon Society. III. Title.
QL405.2.C37 2000
594′.1477—dc21   99-046831

10 9 8 7 6 5 4 3 2   0/0   01   02   03   04
Printed in Hong Kong 54
First printing, July 2000
Front cover photograph: Shells and driftwood, Cape Hatteras National Seashore, North Carolina, by A. Blake Gardner
National Audubon Society® is a registered trademark of National Audubon Society, Inc., all rights reserved.

Contents

Atlantic Giant Cockle page 63

About this book

Whether you see a snail in your own backyard, a chiton at the seashore, or a mussel by a lakeside, this book will help you learn to look at shells the way a naturalist does. The book is divided into four parts:

PART 1: The world of shells

gives you lots of interesting information, such as how and why mollusks make shells, how they are named, and what these incredibly diverse creatures have in common.

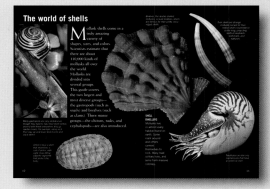

The world of shells

Mollusk shells come in a truly amazing variety of shapes, sizes, and colors. Scientists estimate that there are about 110,000 kinds of mollusks all over the world. Mollusks are divided into several groups. This guide covers the two largest and most diverse groups—the gastropods (such as snails and bivalves (such as clams). Three minor groups—the chitons, tusks, and cephalopods—are also introduced.

PART 2: How to look at shells

tells you what you need to know to begin identifying shells—including what they look like, how mollusks use them, and where you can find them.

Locomotion

Many mollusks are notoriously slow movers, inching along at a "snail's pace." But there are mollusks that can jet-propel themselves through the water or burrow themselves into the sand with surprising speed. Mollusks can get around in a lot of interesting ways, such as gliding, floating, digging, plowing, or hitchhiking.

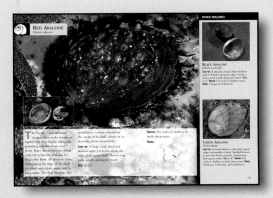

PART 3: The field guide includes detailed descriptions, range maps, and dramatic photographs of 50 common North American shells. In addition, this section provides helpful shorter descriptions accompanied by photographs of more than 100 other important species.

PART 4: The reference section at the back of the book includes a helpful glossary of terms used by naturalists when they talk about shells; lists of useful books, Web sites, and organizations; and an index of species covered in the field guide.

What is a naturalist?

A naturalist is a person who studies nature. Some naturalists are scientists, but others are just people who take pleasure in observing animals and plants in the wild. Scientists who study mollusks, soft-bodied animals that typically make shells, are called malacologists (pronounced mal-uh-KOLL-oh-jists). Scientists who concentrate on the shells of mollusks are called conchologists (kon-KOLL-oh-jists).

R. Tucker Abbott (1919–1995) found his first shells on the beaches of Cape Cod, Massachusetts, when he was a little boy. He grew up to be a world-famous malacologist and conchologist. Abbott shared his knowledge and enthusiasm by writing dozens of books and hundreds of articles about shells. He founded the Bailey-Matthews Shell Museum in Sanibel, Florida, which is the first museum in the world dedicated exclusively to shells and the animals that make them.

YOU CAN BE A NATURALIST, TOO!

Most malacologists and conchologists begin their careers just as R. Tucker Abbott did—as young naturalists who explore the beaches, lakesides, riverbanks, and woodlands around them and become fascinated with the shells they find there. You can be a naturalist, too, by exploring the world around you and reading books about nature.

ESSENTIAL EQUIPMENT

When you go looking for shells, you need a few basic tools. Bring your field guide to help you identify the shells you spot. Always take along a notebook and pencil to record what you see. Writing field notes and making sketches is an important part of being a naturalist. For collecting shells, bring a cloth bag or plastic bucket as well as some small plastic (not glass) jars or small, reclosable bags for shells that are especially small or fragile. You should leave any living mollusks where you find them and sketch pictures or take photographs of these creatures instead. If you bring along a magnifying glass, you can get a close-up look at things you find. Wear boots or an old pair of sneakers that you can get wet.

Rules for shell-collecting and mollusk-watching

- When you go out exploring, take a friend along and tell a grown-up where you are going.

- Be careful when climbing around on rocks, jetties, or reefs.

- Wear shoes that protect your feet.

- Always put back rocks or other objects you might move while searching for mollusks.

- Respect the animals that make shells. Collect only empty shells, and never remove live mollusks from their homes.

- Do not collect more shells than you really need or want. Leave some where you find them for other shell collectors.

- Share your shells, notes, photos, and drawings with friends, family, and teachers. Everyone loves shells!

What are shells?

Shells are the protective coverings that animals called mollusks—such as clams, snails, and oysters—make to protect their soft bodies. Vertebrates—that is, mammals, fishes, birds, reptiles, and amphibians—have an internal skeleton, a bony frame that supports and protects soft tissue. Mollusks are invertebrates and don't have bones. Instead, they have a fortresslike external skeleton—their shell.

Mollusks, unlike crabs and lobsters, never shed their shells. A mollusk and its shell go hand-in-hand from birth to death. If a shell gets broken, the mollusk has to do its best to repair the crack. Repaired shells are fairly easy to find. Look for dark, jagged lines like the mended cracks on this snail shell.

HOW ARE SHELLS MADE?

Mollusks have a special shell-making organ called the mantle, which is a fleshy sheet that surrounds the mollusk's body like a cape. Mollusks take in minerals and gases when they feed and breathe. Two of these, calcium (a mineral) and carbon dioxide (a gas), are used to make layers of calcium carbonate crystals, which build up to form the shell.

Some mollusks, like the Colorful Moon Snail (page 103), can extend their mantle outside their shell. But in most mollusks the mantle is usually hidden away inside the shell.

mantle

HOW DO SHELLS GROW?

Mollusk shells grow from their leading edge outward. Shell growth happens in stages, and each growth spurt is usually marked by a strong line, known as a growth line. Many species of mollusks stop growing once they have reached maturity, which may take several years.

leading edge

growth lines

Right: As the Lightning Whelk (page 112) grows, the coloration and spiral shape of its shell become more defined. Left: The spiral is clearly visible when the mature shell is viewed from above.

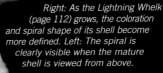

11

The world of shells

Mollusk shells come in a truly amazing variety of shapes, sizes, and colors. Scientists estimate that there are about 110,000 kinds of mollusks all over the world. Mollusks are divided into several groups. This guide covers the two largest and most diverse groups— the gastropods (such as snails) and bivalves (such as clams). Three minor groups—the chitons, tusks, and cephalopods—are also introduced.

Many gastropods are very mobile even though they have to haul their shell homes around with them everywhere they go. Garden snails, for example, easily inch their way up and down tree trunks and plant stems.

Chitons have a shell that resembles a suit of armor, with eight close-fitting, platelike segments that protect the body.

Bivalves, the double-shelled mollusks, include scallops, which are famous for their pretty, wavy-edged shells.

Tusk shells are strange mollusks named for their hollow shell's resemblance to the long, projecting teeth of elephants, wild boars, and walruses.

SHELL DWELLERS

Mollusks live in almost every habitat found on earth. Some roam around and others cement themselves to rock. Many lead solitary lives, and some form massive colonies.

Nautiluses are the only cephalopods that have an external shell.

Western Ribbed Top Shells page 85

What's in a name?

Scientists put all animals into groups. Every animal is part of the animal kingdom. Within the animal kingdom, all mollusks are grouped into the mollusk phylum. The mollusk phylum is broken down into several classes: gastropods, bivalves, cephalopods, chitons, and tusks. Each class is separated into orders, and each order into families. Each family is divided into genera (plural of genus), which are subdivided into species.

RULES OF THE NAME GAME

Living creatures have a variety of names. When a scientist discovers a new species of animal, it is given a scientific name. Scientific names have two parts, the genus and the species, in that order. Some creatures, such as the famous dinosaur *Tyrannosaurus rex,* are known only by their scientific names. Most familiar animals, though, are better known by their common names. For instance, *Felis catus* is known as the house cat and *Helix aspersa* is known as the Brown Garden Snail. Many species are known by more than one common name.

Several species of wentletraps are commonly found on North American beaches. Look for shells that resemble tiny spiral staircases.

TWO MOLLUSKS CLASSIFIED

Notice that the Queen Conch and the Atlantic Calico Scallop both belong to the animal kingdom and share the same phylum, Mollusca. However, the similarity ends there. The two mollusks belong to different classes, orders, families, genera, and species.

Kingdom	Animalia	Kingdom	Animalia
Phylum	Mollusca	Phylum	Mollusca
Class	Gastropoda	Class	Bivalvia
Order	Neotaenioglossa	Order	Ostreoida
Family	Strombidae	Family	Pectinidae
Genus	*Strombus*	Genus	*Argopecten*
Species	*gigas*	Species	*gibbus*
(Queen Conch)		(Atlantic Calico Scallop)	

A SNAIL BY ANY OTHER NAME

Many mollusks have names that describe their shell. The wentletraps (left) are a family of mollusks whose name comes from the Dutch word for "spiral staircase." The Bleeding Tooth (right) has bright orange-red teeth at the edge of the shell opening.

If you are on a rocky beach in Florida and find a snail shell that looks like it has bloody teeth, it's a good bet you've actually found a Bleeding Tooth shell (page 86).

Gastropods

Gastropods are the largest group of mollusks, and their variety of shapes, sizes, and colors is astounding. Snails and slugs are gastropods, and so are limpets, abalones, worm shells, rock shells, and many others.

GASTROPOD VARIETY

Malacologists don't agree on exactly how many different kinds of gastropods exist. There may be more than 50,000 species worldwide, several thousand of which can be found in North America.

Giant Keyhole Limpet page 83

GASTROPODS ARE EVERYWHERE

Gastropods live in fresh and salt water as well as on land. They have adapted to just about every habitat found on earth. You can find gastropods all over North America—cruising through mud in the dark depths of the sea; riding ocean waves on air bubbles; stuck to the undersides of lily pads floating in quiet ponds; inching along tree branches; munching away at garden plants; or crawling through leaf litter on forest floors.

Flamingo Tongue page 105

Gastropods move around on a large, muscular foot. Watch a snail such as the Grove Snail (page 148) chew its way across a leaf and you'll see how well these animals are named: Gastropod means "stomach-footed" in Latin.

Most gastropods have eyes on or near tentacles on the head. The Queen Conch (page 100) peeks out of its shell with bright eyes on the tips of little stalks.

GASTROPOD REPRODUCTION

Most gastropods lay eggs. Depending on the species, the female produces hundreds to millions of eggs, which may form strands, towers, or large jellylike masses. In saltwater species, the young normally hatch as tiny, free-swimming larvae. In freshwater and land species, the young may do more of their developing within the egg and then hatch fully formed.

Kellet's Whelk (page 115) laying eggs

There are thousands of bivalves of all sizes and shapes in the world. The Giant Clam (top) is huge compared to the tiny Purple Gem Clam (bottom), but both are bivalves.

Bivalves

Bivalves are mollusks that have two shells, or valves. The familiar clams, scallops, mussels, and oysters, as well as ark shells, jingle shells, and jewel boxes, are all bivalves. This name makes a lot of sense for these double-shelled creatures: The word *bivalve* comes from the Latin word for "folding doors."

Blue Mussels page 52

Leafy Jewel Box page 61

BIVALVE HOMES

Bivalves live in water—fresh or salt—but never on land. A few swim freely, but most tend to stay put once they've plastered themselves to rocks, piers, or coral reefs; burrowed under sand or mud; or drilled into clay, rock, or wood.

Atlantic Giant Cockle
page 63

Mussels releasing eggs and sperm

BIVALVE REPRODUCTION

Most bivalves reproduce by releasing eggs and sperm into the water. The young then hatch as tiny larvae that swim about until their shells are developed enough for them to settle into the sand, mud, rock, or other surface.

Most bivalves don't have eyes, but scallops do. The Atlantic Bay Scallop (page 58) has about a hundred tiny, bright eyes lining the mantle tissue at the edge of its shell.

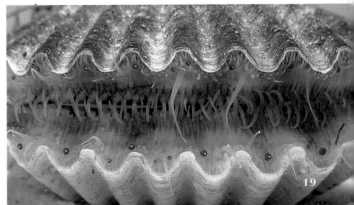

19

Gastropod and bivalve design

Most of the world's mollusks are either gastropods or bivalves. It is easy to tell the difference between a gastropod and a bivalve if you know their basic characteristics.

GASTROPOD ANATOMY

The typical gastropod has a flexible body that can be extended out of and pulled back into a shell; a large foot to move around on; and tentacles, which are often on the head.

tentacle

head

whorl

spire

apex

foot

GASTROPOD SHELLS

Most gastropod shells are coiled, or whorled, into a spiral formation. The overall shape of gastropod shells ranges from nearly flat to turban-shaped to tall and cone-shaped.

The surface of a gastropod shell can be smooth or elaborately textured with raised ribs, etched lines, soft folds, sharp spines, blunt knobs, or tiny, beadlike bumps. The Lace Murex (page 106) has lacy frills.

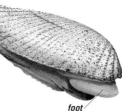

siphon

foot

BIVALVE BODIES

Bivalves have a headless body with a muscular foot, which in many species is hatchet-shaped and makes a great tool for burrowing into sand or mud. Bivalves have snorkel-like tubes called siphons for feeding and breathing, and for releasing waste.

BIVALVE SHELLS

A bivalve's two shells (valves) are connected by a hinge and held together on the inside by tough tissues and large muscles. Many species have teeth in the hinge to help keep the shells tightly closed.

hinge

teeth

valve

Left: The surface of a bivalve shell is often marked with fine growth lines that form a concentric pattern like the bands of color in a rainbow, as in the Northern Quahog (page 64).

Right: Ribs on a bivalve shell, such as the Atlantic Bay Scallop (page 58), form a radiating pattern similar to the folds in a paper fan.

rib

growth line

Chitons, tusks, and cephalopods

W hile gastropods and bivalves are found across the continent, chitons, tusks, and cephalopods live only in marine (ocean) waters. Their fascinating shells do not show up in as many collections because they can be difficult to find.

valve

mantle (or girdle)

Underside view of empty Lined Red Chiton shell page 132

Top view of Lined Red Chiton page 132

CHITONS

Chitons have eight valves, or shells, which fit so tightly together that at first glance chitons appear to have a single shell. The chiton's mantle surrounds the eight valves and holds them together. It is so good at holding things in place it is often called a girdle. Most chitons are oval in shape, although some can be quite narrow. Chitons live only in salt water, where they typically cling tightly to rocks. In areas where they are common, live chitons are easy to observe, but their empty shells rarely wash up on shore.

TUSKS

Tusk shells are curious creatures that live on the ocean bottom with the large end of their shell stuck down into the sand or mud and the narrow end sticking up into the water. A great many of the world's several hundred kinds of tusk shells live in deep offshore waters, and their shells rarely end up on beaches. Only a few species are common in shallower waters.

Ivory Tusk Shells
page 129

Ram's Horn
page 135

CEPHALOPODS

North American cephalopods include squids, octopuses, argonauts, and spirulas. With tentacle arms and large eyes, they actively pursue their animal prey. Cephalopods in our range have no outer shell, but they do have a variety of shell-like structures that they leave behind: The squidlike Common Spirula has a spiral-shaped internal shell called the Ram's Horn; argonauts make delicate spiral cases to hold their eggs. Cephalopod "shells" arrive on beaches after storm waves and winds blow them in from deep offshore waters.

Diet

In the world of mollusks there are vegetarians (plant eaters), carnivores (meat eaters), and scavengers (which eat scraps of dead matter). Most mollusks are slow-moving, so they have devised ways of catching their meals that do not require speed—and some eat without really moving at all.

Queen Conch (page 100) feeding on seaweed

EATING TOOLS

Gastropods, chitons, tusks, and cephalopods—that is, all mollusks except bivalves—have an organ in the mouth called the radula (pronounced RAD-yoo-luh), with rows of tiny teeth. Different species use the radula to collect food in various ways, ranging from picking up bits of debris to preying on animals.

Cones have a special harpoon-shaped radula that they use to spear marine worms and small fishes. Deadly barbs on the radula hold the cone's prey and inject it with poison at the same time. This cone is feeding on a goby fish.

Whelks prey on sea urchins and anemones (marine invertebrates), using the radula to tear off big pieces of the victim.

Land snails munch on all sorts of vegetation, nibbling away at living and dead material they find in their path. This Florida Tree Snail (page 144) is eating lichen off a tree trunk.

SIPHON-FEEDING

Bivalves use snorkel-like tubes called siphons to feed, either by sucking in water and straining out tiny food particles or by vacuuming up tiny food bits from the pond, lake, or ocean bottom.

Variable Coquinas (page 68) follow the tides in order to stay in areas with breaking waves, which churn up food particles for them to eat.

Blue Mussels (page 52) form large colonies on coastal rocks where waves wash over them, bringing a steady supply of microscopic food matter.

25

Defense

Mollusks don't make their shells for people to collect. They grow them because their soft bodies need protection— from the weather and from the predators that want to eat them. Most mollusks have a shell big enough so that the animal can pull its body away from the shell edge, at least a little bit, if danger threatens. Here are some other ways in which shells protect the mollusks that live in them.

The larger a shell is, the fewer predators there are that will disturb it. Not many creatures can successfully attack a full-grown conch, some of which, such as the Queen Conch (page 100), can have foot-high shells.

Brown Garden Snail (page 149) blends in with rock

CAMOUFLAGE

If a shell looks enough like its surroundings, predators may have a hard time finding it. Many kinds of land snails blend in with the ground, where they spend most of their time.

Atlantic Thorny Oyster page 61

KNOBS AND SPINES

Large knobs projecting from a shell's surface make it seem larger than it is and also make it more difficult to swallow. If blunt knobs are bad news for a potential predator, imagine what an obstacle the sharp spines on an Atlantic Thorny Oyster must be!

True Tulip (page 117) pulling shut its operculum to keep predators out

BARRIERS
Many snails have a trapdoorlike operculum that they can close over the shell opening. Many land snails, cowries, and nerites have a number of teeth to guard the opening.

SLIPPERY SURFACES
Olives and cowries have such smoothly polished shells that they can often slip out of the grasp of crabs and other marine animals that hunt them.

Chestnut Cowrie page 105

RIBS, RIDGES, AND CORDS
Ribs, ridges, and cords help make a shell stronger and more difficult for predators to break into. The shells of cockles, scallops, neptunes, limpets, and some freshwater mussels are all strengthened with ribs (which run lengthwise), ridges (which go across a shell), or cords (which wrap around a shell).

The New England Neptune (page 114) has thick, spiral cords that strengthen the shell.

Predators

Shells can protect mollusks in many ways, but most mollusks are small and slow, and there are a lot of bigger and faster predators that want to eat them. It can be difficult for a snail or clam to make a getaway. Mollusks also have to watch out for predators among their own kind.

MAMMAL MENACE

Raccoons, muskrats, and river otters bite into freshwater mussels and snails or pull them apart. Sea otters dive down and pry abalones and other kinds of marine mollusks off underwater rocks. After it breaks open the thick shell, the otter feasts on the mollusk while floating on its back.

Sea otter feeding on a bivalve

Whelks attacking each other

BREAK-INS

Some large sea snails, including whelks and tulip shells, use the outer lip of their shell to pry open the shells of clams and other bivalves—or to attack each other. Certain rock shells also use their shells as weapons. The shells are equipped with a sharp spine on the outer lip. This can chip away at and eventually open clams and barnacles.

DEADLY HUGS

Sea stars will grab hold of a clam or scallop and pull on the two valves with their many arms until the mollusk's muscles finally tire. The shells have to open only a little way for the sea star to consume its bivalve dinner.

Sea star feeding on a clam

BOMBS AWAY!

Gulls are well known for carrying clams and snails in their beaks and dropping them onto parking lots and roads in order to break the shells and feed on the meat inside.

Moon snail drilling another large sea snail

IT'S A MOLLUSK-EAT-MOLLUSK WORLD

When you find a shell with a perfectly round hole in it, you can be almost sure that it was made by a predatory moon snail or drill snail. These snails use their rasping tongue, or radula, and shell-dissolving juices to drill holes through the shells of other mollusks—a slow process that can take several days. When the drilling is finally complete, the snail feeds on its prey.

Shells as homes for other creatures

Snail with seaweed growing on it

Mollusks make shells to live in, but somewhere along the line many shells end up being homes for other creatures. Both the outside and inside of a shell can serve as a living area for various plant and animal species, often while the mollusk inside is still alive.

HITCHHIKERS

Shells are hard, and hard surfaces attract animals and plants that need a place to settle and grow. Barnacles, sponges, corals, seaweeds, and small encrusting animals called bryozoans are some types of marine life found on shells. Quite often these hitchhikers help to camouflage the mollusk shells underneath.

Clam and thorny oyster attached to each other

HANGERS-ON

Many kinds of mollusks—such as jingle shells, thorny oysters, slipper shells, cup-and-saucer shells, and worm shells—attach themselves to other mollusks.

Scaled Worm Shells (page 92) on an abalone

HOUSEMATES

Some animals and plants share the homes of living mollusks. Slipper shells will sometimes take up residence inside whelks. Algae can grow within a live bivalve. Conchfishes make their homes in living conchs, coming out to feed only at night.

Conchfish at home in a Queen Conch (page 100)

HERMIT HOMES

Hermit crabs are probably the best-known inhabitants of empty shells. In all sorts of salt water, soft-bodied hermit crabs search out and find empty snail and tusk shells for their homes. As they grow, hermit crabs need to change their shell homes to fit their expanding bodies. Look in the shallows to see hermit crabs scurrying about in their chosen shells. If you watch closely, you may see a hermit crab change shells right before your eyes.

Hermit crab in the broken shell of a moon snail

Locomotion

Many mollusks are notoriously slow movers, inching along at a "snail's pace." But there are mollusks that can jet-propel themselves through the water or burrow themselves into the sand with surprising speed. Mollusks can get around in a lot of interesting ways, such as gliding, floating, digging, plowing, or hitchhiking.

FOOT TRAFFIC

For most mollusks, getting around involves using a large and muscular foot. A snail's foot muscles spread out and contract in waves and move the snail along whether it's crawling on the ground or gliding through the water. Bivalves typically move by extending the hatchet-shaped foot up through mud or sand, expanding the end of it, and then contracting the muscles to pull themselves upward.

Woodland snail

SHELL-PROPELLED

Scallops are surprisingly swift, jetting through the water by opening and closing their shells and shooting out water. They can move forward, backward, or sideways, depending on which way they squirt out the water.

Scallop fleeing a sea star's deadly grasp

Periiwinkle inching across the beach, leaving a long "footprint" behind

ALL ABOARD!

Slipper shells perch atop a big whelk or moon snail and let the larger mollusk carry them around. Shipworms and other borers may bore (drill) into a loose piece of wood that floats hundreds or even thousands of miles on ocean currents, carrying these mollusks all around the world.

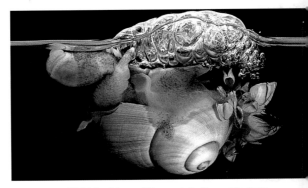

The Common Violet Snail (page 96) spends its life upside down, attached to the underside of a raft of bubbles. It depends on ocean currents and waves to move it around with the jellyfish it eats.

Where to look for shells and mollusks

Observing a land snail

Whether you are looking under logs for land snails, scouring the seashore for marine shells, or pawing through pond muck for freshwater shells, you need to know where, how, and when to look. The next nine pages show you some places to look for living mollusks (to observe) and empty mollusk shells (to collect) and provide pointers to help make your field trips successful.

RANGES AND HABITATS

Knowing where particular mollusk species live can help you identify the mollusks and shells that you find. Field guides like this one tell you two things about where a mollusk lives: its range and its habitat. A mollusk's range is the geographic area where it can be found, such as Alaska or the Gulf of Mexico. The habitat is the type of environment a species of mollusk lives in. A species' habitat, whether on land or in water, has to offer just the right living conditions. For a marine species, key conditions that determine whether a particular place is a good living environment are: the temperature of the water, the amount of salt and oxygen in the water, and how much the water moves.

Black Top Shell's range

EMPTIES

You can expect to find empty shells near the living mollusk's habitat, but don't be surprised to find them in many other habitats as well. Empty shells can get carried all over the place by water, wind, hermit crabs, and predators.

Black Top Shells (page 85) in their habitat

Looking on land

Gastropods are the only mollusks that live on land. Looking for land snails and collecting their empty shells can be lots of fun. Even though many species are quite small, land snails come in a nice assortment of shapes, colors, and sizes. They have adapted to just about every habitat on earth, including deserts and mountains, but you can find lots of them in your own backyard or local park and many more in any of North America's various types of woodlands. Many kinds of snails love damp places, so be on the lookout in basements and greenhouses.

Garden snails in flowerpot

GARDENS

Gardens attract many kinds of gastropods, including slugs. Slugs are detested by many people who would probably not mind them as much if they had a shell covering their glistening body. Some snails that do have shells and live in flower and vegetable gardens are Grove Snails and Brown Garden Snails. Most gardeners will be happy to let you collect snails in their gardens, since most of the snails are there to eat the plants that gardeners are working so hard to grow. By moving any living snails you find to nearby areas outside the garden, you can do the gardener a favor without harming the snails.

WOODLANDS

Woodlands are good places to start your search for land shells. Snails are seldom sitting right out in the open, as most are nocturnal (active at nighttime), so be prepared to turn a lot of things over. When you roll logs and flip boards over looking for snails, you may find ants, centipedes, millipedes, salamanders, sow bugs, and all sorts of other creatures sharing these dark hiding places. Forest snails can get quite large and are frequently found under logs and bark. Sift carefully through leaf litter for Forest Disk Snails and other tiny, intricate species.

LOOK UP!

In Florida especially, don't forget to look up in trees and shrubs for climbing snails.

Florida Tree Snails page 144

Looking in freshwater habitats

They may be buried in muddy and sandy bottoms or clinging to lily pads and cattail stems, but there are all sorts of snails and bivalves just waiting to be discovered in freshwater habitats all over North America. The quietest ponds and the swiftest rivers have mollusks, from tiny fingernail clams to giant freshwater mussels.

RIVERS AND STREAMS

Rivers and streams have flowing water. Rivers are generally larger and faster-moving than streams. Some rivers are home to multitudes of mussels, whose shells range from beautiful to grotesque. There are mussel shells so big and sharp-edged that they are known as "heel splitters." Remember to wear old sneakers to protect your feet.

Pond with log and lily pads

PONDS

Ponds are shallow, calm bodies of fresh water that often have abundant vegetation along the edges or even across the whole surface.

Pend Oreille Lake, Idaho Panhandle National Forest

LAKES

Lakes are usually larger and deeper than ponds and tend to have extensive areas of open water. Most vegetation in lakes is very close to the shore.

CAUTION!

It can be great fun to wade in when looking for freshwater shells, but don't go too deep into ponds and lakes, and stick to the shoreline and shallows of rivers and streams, which can have fast and tricky currents. Never walk on frozen mud or ice; they may look solid, but they can easily give way under you.

Florida Apple Snail page 142

Tips

- Look first along the water's edge to find empty shells that may have floated up to the shoreline. You can collect and identify these shells and learn about some of the species that share that particular habitat.

- Check docks, floats, fallen branches, floating logs, and rocks for living snails of all sorts.

- Carefully examine vegetation; you may find freshwater limpets and other interesting species anchored to the undersides of lily pads, and many snails will climb along stems of water plants.

- Use a sturdy net to dig into the mud, sand, or gravel bottom and see what's living down below. Scoop in open areas as well as down in the muck around the roots of plants.

Looking for marine shells

No place is more satisfying to look for shells and mollusks than the beach. On great days, there are so many shells it is hard to know where to look first. On not-so-great days, you can still enjoy the waves, the sand and rocks, and the birds. Here are some of the best marine habitats for shell-collecting and mollusk-watching.

DRIFTLINES

Driftlines, the wavy lines of ocean debris that you find on the upper part of any beach, are not a habitat for living mollusks, but they are a great place to start shell-collecting. Everything that floats in on high tides gets deposited in the driftline. Much of what you'll find here— including seaweeds, dead crabs, and sometimes jellyfishes—once lived elsewhere and got uprooted, died, or otherwise left its chosen habitat and was swept ashore by the waves. The shells you find here may be perfect or they may be worn and broken. Remember to look under and on driftwood and seaweed. Below the main driftline may be other finer lines, sometimes containing multitudes of tiny shells. Crouch down and have a look at these. You can fill a plastic bag or cup with some fine drift material and sort it out at home. You may find thousands of tiny shells in just one quart of drift!

Driftline at Cumberland Island, Georgia

Tidepool in coastal Washington state

Looking in a tidepool

TIDEPOOLS

Tidepools, pockets of seawater that are left in rocky areas when the tide goes out, are fascinating marine communities. Limpets, keyhole limpets, abalones, rock snails, nerites, periwinkles, top shells, chitons, mussels, and many other mollusks live here. So do sea stars, sea urchins, sea anemones, seaweeds, and much more. All tidepool residents have to be able to cope with the constant change from being submerged under water to being exposed to open air. You need to be at the ocean at low tide to study tidepools. The best tidepools are those that are completely cut off from the waves by large rocks. This makes the pools quiet and easy to look into.

IN THE ZONE

A tremendous number of mollusks live in the intertidal zone, the area between the highest and lowest points that the tides reach each day. The waves bring great quantities of food and oxygen here. The only problem is that for at least part of every day, the tide goes out. To shelter themselves from the sun and the wind, mollusks burrow down under the mud and sand (clams), close themselves up tightly in their shells (periwinkles), or clamp themselves down into rocky crevices (chitons and limpets) to await the incoming tide.

Salt marsh, Chincoteague National Wildlife Refuge, Virginia

SALT MARSHES

Salt marshes are habitats where fresh water from land meets salt water from the ocean. Marsh trips are best done at low tide. Streams and inlets cut into the marsh in places and expose banks of mud and clay. Look here for mussels, marsh clams, boring clams, periwinkles, and saltmarsh snails. Marsh mud can be very sticky, so take a friend along on marsh trips (and on any trip where there's a lot of mud around) so that you have help getting your feet unstuck.

San Luis Obispo, California

PIERS

Wooden piers and stone pilings host seaweeds, barnacles, urchins, sea stars, sea squirts, and all manner of fascinating animal and plant life. Squeezed in among these can be a great array of mollusks, including snails, bivalves, and chitons aplenty. Of course, the parts of these structures that teem with life are usually covered at high tide. Do your pier peering at the lowest tide.

SANDFLATS AND MUDFLATS

On flat beaches, low tide exposes wide areas of sand or mud. Look for moon snails, horn snails, olives, venus clams, razor clams, tellins, and other mollusks crawling about or resting just below the surface. Almost all of the mollusks that live here go under the sand or mud when the tide goes out. If you look for them at low tide, watch for small telltale mounds or bumps where snails have buried themselves just under the surface. Also watch for the siphon holes of clams and other bivalves. Dig down a little to the side of the hole to unearth the shell without breaking it. You can search a mud- or sandflat when it is covered with water by using a glass-bottomed viewing box or a mask and snorkel. You are bound to see more mollusk activity when the tide is in and the animals are moving about and feeding.

Mudflats at Hunting Island State Park, South Carolina

Collecting marine shells

Beachcombing tips

• Try to plan your ocean trips to coincide with low tides. This widens the beach and exposes habitats that are usually under water. At certain times of the month, tides are especially low. Check tide schedules under the weather forecast in local newspapers.

• If you want an uncrowded shelling experience, try to visit the ocean on weekdays or during seasons when the shores are least crowded.

• If possible, get to the beach soon after stormy weather. Many choice and otherwise rarely found shells get thrown up on beaches after storms.

Keeping a shell collection

O nce you have gone out and found shells, you can take them home, clean them up, and organize them into a shell collection. A good shell collection is something you and your family will be proud of. Follow the steps on these pages to get your shell collection started.

Collecting and organizing shells

STEP 1: CLEANING

If you have collected completely empty shells, cleaning them is as easy as rinsing them with fresh water, scraping away barnacles and other unwanted shell growth, and letting them dry. If you found shells that have dead mollusks inside them, rinse them out or let them sit overnight in fresh water and then rinse them out under a strong faucet.

Conus ermineus Born, 1778
From sand/eel grass, 25' water.
Young Island, St. Vincent,
W. I., August, 1992.

Cone shell with a data card

STEP 2: ORGANIZING

Shell collections can be organized in any number of ways. For example, you can group your shells by family, putting all mussels in one section and all moon snails in another, and so on. You can group your shells according to where you found them, with all of the shells found at a particular beach, pond, or woodland kept together. Make little data cards to go with your shells. Include the name of the shell, where you found it, and the date it was found. These can be handwritten or typed on a school or home computer.

Above: Variety of shells on display

Below: Old cigar boxes are perfect for storing shells. Individual plastic boxes lined with cotton keep fragile shells extra safe. Pictured is a carefully stored collection of wentletraps.

DON'T OVERCOLLECT

When you go shelling, try to remember which species you have at home. Better yet, take along a list of what you already have. Keep only the best shells you find and leave the rest for someone else to discover.

Conservation

Humans share the environment with all living things. Unfortunately, people have not always respected the natural world. They have dumped waste in the wild and have taken over habitats that were once homes for plants and animals. Many populations of freshwater and marine mollusks are threatened because of pollution, loss of habitat, introduction of foreign species, and over-harvesting for food. Governments make laws to protect the natural world. You can do your part by respecting the environment and getting involved with conservation organizations.

Queen Conch page 100

COLLECTING

When you are looking for shells to add to your collection, it's important that you leave living mollusks where you find them. Strict laws protect some species, such as the Queen Conch. So many people have collected the living mollusk for its beautiful shell that there are not many left for others to enjoy.

Banbury Springs Limpet

THREATENED AND ENDANGERED SPECIES

Every plant or animal that is in danger of disappearing from the earth needs protection. That includes California Condors, Red Wolves, and rare and threatened mollusks. The Banbury Springs Limpet, found in springs that feed the Snake River in Idaho, has been placed on the U.S. Federal Endangered Species List. Its habitat has been threatened by development. Laws such as the U.S. Endangered Species Act are helping to protect its survival by preserving its habitat. Now this unique and beautiful gastropod is on the comeback trail because people got involved to save it. Still at risk are many other mollusks, including about half of North America's 300 or so species of freshwater mussels.

Zebra Mussels (page 139) attached to a clam

INTRODUCED SPECIES

Sometimes mollusks are threatened by the introduction of foreign species. Originally from Asia, the Zebra Mussel made its way into North American waters on ships. Zebra Mussels attach themselves to native clams and other mussels, depriving them of food and oxygen. Zebra Mussels are a nuisance for people, too, clogging water pipes and dams, causing serious and expensive problems.

Using the field guide

This section features 50 common North American shells and includes brief descriptions of 101 more. Color photographs and details about each shell are included to help you identify it.

Lewis's Moon Snail
page 102

Saltwater species are covered first, then freshwater species, then land species. Within these general categories, the shells are grouped by class, beginning with bivalves. Shells appearing on facing pages are either related or share some traits or characteristics.

SHELL I.D. TIPS

- The appearance of a shell may change when the animal living inside it dies.
- Many shells have a skinlike coating that is often a different color than the bare shell. The skin may peel off as the shell dries.
- Shells may be covered with seaweed, mud, sand, or dirt.
- Many shells lose their shine if they have been lying on a beach or pond shoreline or under a bleaching sun.

ICONS

These icons appear on each left-hand page in the field guide. They identify a shell's general shape and category.

Bivalve

Cephalopod

Gastropod

Chiton

Tusk

SHAPE ICON
This icon identifies the featured shell's general shape and category.

BOX HEADING
The box heading alerts you to other shells covered in the box that are similar to the main shell on the page.

NAME
Each shell's common and scientific names appear here.

🐚 RED ABALONE
Haliotis rufescens

The Pacific Coast abalones cling to their rocky homes so tightly that they hardly notice the pounding surf that flows over them. Brave divers swim in strong currents to harvest abalones for their tasty flesh. All abalones have holes along the edge of the shell to inhale and exhale water and to pass waste. The Red Abalone, like its relatives, is most colorful on the inside of its shell, where its iridescence shines beautifully.

Look for: A large, oval, deep red abalone with 3–4 holes along the edge of the wavy shell. Shimmering pink, pearly, and green inside. **Size:** 8–12".

Habitat: On rocks in shallow to fairly deep water.

Range:

BLACK ABALONE
Haliotis cracherodii
Look for: A smooth, round, black abalone with 5–8 holes along the edge. Inside is silvery with a pink and green sheen. **Size:** 5–6". **Habitat:** On rocks in shallow water **Range:** Oregon to California.

GREEN ABALONE
Haliotis fulgens
Look for: A round abalone with many spiral ridges and usually 6 holes. Reddish-brown to greenish-brown outside, shimmering blue-green inside. **Size:** 6–8". **Habitat:** On rocks in shallow to fairly deep water. **Range:** Monterey, California, and southward.

79

INSET PHOTO
On some pages, an inset photo shows another view of the shell. For example, on a page where the main photograph shows the living animal, an inset may show the empty shell.

IDENTIFICATION CAPSULE
The identification capsule covers all the details you need to identify a shell: color, shape, size, and other features described in this book. Measurements given for each shell are for the longest part of the shell. Depending on the species, this may be the height, the length, or the width.

RANGE AND HABITAT
The range and habitat listings tell you whether or not a shell is likely to be seen in your area. The habitat information describes where the animal actually lives, not necessarily where you will find its shell.

49

TURKEY WING
Arca zebra

Among the shells that litter southeastern beaches are many single valves of the handsome Turkey Wing. Also known as the Zebra Ark, the Turkey Wing is the only ark shell sporting stripes. All North American ark shells have straight hinges lined with many small teeth and ribs that radiate from the top of the shell. These shells are often worn down in spots or have animals or plants living on them.

LOOK FOR: A long, quite narrow ark shell with brownish zebra stripes; a very long, straight hinge; and numerous ribs. Commonly washed ashore.

BLOOD ARK
Anadara ovalis

LOOK FOR: A rounded ark shell with a dark brown skin and numerous squared-off ribs. This species is named for its red blood; the blood of most mollusks is clear. **SIZE:** 1½–2". **HABITAT:** In sand in shallow water. **RANGE:** Cape Cod to Texas.

PONDEROUS ARK
Noetia ponderosa

LOOK FOR: A thick, heavy, triangular ark shell with strong, flat ribs and large beaks that turn backward. White outside, with dark, velvety skin. **SIZE:** 1½–2½". **HABITAT:** In sand in shallow water. **RANGE:** Virginia to Texas.

SIZE: 2–4".

HABITAT: Attached to rocks in shallow water.

RANGE:

51

BLUE MUSSEL
Mytilus edulis

Shell-seekers will find the Blue Mussel where waves wash over coastal rocks. Many kinds of mussels, including this one, grow in tight clusters or large beds and cover the rocks they cling to. They attach to rocks by strong hairlike strands known as byssal threads.

LOOK FOR: A deep blue to blackish, teardrop-shaped mussel with no ribs. Growth lines are usually visible. Bluish-white inside. Blue Mussels often occur in tremendous numbers, covering tidepools and jetties.

SIZE: 2–3".

HABITAT: On intertidal rocks and pilings.

RANGE:

CALIFORNIA MUSSEL
Mytilus californianus

LOOK FOR: A large, brownish, teardrop-shaped mussel with many ribs. Growth lines are easily seen; apex is usually worn.
SIZE: 4–8". **HABITAT:** On intertidal rocks.
RANGE: Alaska to California.

NORTHERN HORSE MUSSEL
Modiolus modiolus

LOOK FOR: A large, oval, blackish mussel with a thick brown skin. Not as pointed as the Blue Mussel. Often found with seaweed attached to it. **SIZE:** 4–6". **HABITAT:** Sandy bottoms in fairly deep water. **RANGE:** Alaska to California; Arctic to New Jersey.

AMBER PEN SHELL
Pinna carnea

Pen shells—large and distinctly fan-shaped—are unmistakable. Look for them partly buried in the sand or mud, with the narrow end of the shell pointing down and the rounded top sticking up slightly above the surface (as pictured in the large photograph above). When a tropical storm hits, thousands and thousands of pen shells get pulled from the sea bottom and end up on south Florida beaches. Many collectors consider the Amber Pen Shell the most beautiful shell of its kind.

LOOK FOR: An amber-colored pen shell with or without many rows of small spines.

SAW-TOOTHED PEN SHELL
Atrina serrata

LOOK FOR: A light brown pen shell with about 30 rows of very small scales. **SIZE:** 8–12". **HABITAT:** Sandy and muddy bottoms in shallow water. **RANGE:** North Carolina to Florida; Texas.

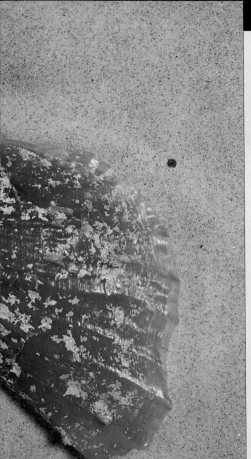

SIZE: 6–10".

HABITAT: Sand, sandy mud, and gravel bottoms in shallow water.

RANGE:

STIFF PEN SHELL
Atrina rigida

LOOK FOR: A dark brown pen shell with about half as many rows of scales as the Saw-toothed Pen Shell, but with each scale much larger. **SIZE:** 6–11". **HABITAT:** Sand, mud, and gravel bottoms in shallow water. **RANGE:** North Carolina to Florida.

EASTERN OYSTER
Crassostrea virginica

If you walk among the oysters in a colony, make sure your feet are protected: The edges of oyster shells are sharp and can cut your feet. Oysters are among the great delicacies eaten by shellfish-lovers all over the world. Unfortunately, a great number of Eastern Oyster colonies have been devastated by water pollution.

Look for: A chalky white to light gray, thick-shelled bivalve. White with purple stain inside. May be oval, long and slender, or almost round. Some contain gem-quality pearls.

Size: 3–8".

Habitat: Attached to hard surfaces in quiet, shallow water.

Range:

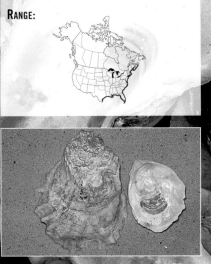

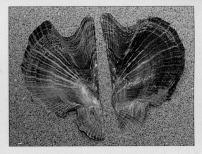

ATLANTIC WINGED OYSTER
Pteria columbus

Look for: An oyster with a long wing along the hinge. Pearly inside. **Size:** 1½–3".
Habitat: On sea whips in water 10–100' deep. **Range:** North Carolina to Florida.

PACIFIC OYSTER
Crassostrea gigas

Look for: A large, strongly ribbed oyster similar to the Eastern Oyster. **Size:** 6–10".
Habitat: Attached to hard surfaces or each other in intertidal zone. **Range:** British Columbia to northern California.

ATLANTIC BAY SCALLOP
Argopecten irradians

Nothing else looks quite like a scallop, with its rounded shape and triangular "wings" on either side of the beak. While young Atlantic Bay Scallops can be quite colorful, larger, older shells are usually not very flashy. Adult scallops can jet themselves around by opening and closing their valves, rapidly forcing water out from between the wings. A row of well-developed eyes lines the scallop's mantle.

LOOK FOR: A round, rather drab scallop (though young specimens may be orange or yellow) with fairly inflated valves, 12–21 strong ribs, and wings that are equal in size. May have bands of color.

ATLANTIC CALICO SCALLOP
Argopecten gibbus

LOOK FOR: A small, brightly colored scallop. Colors range from yellow to purplish, with darker blotches. Valves are inflated, with equal wings and 19–21 ribs. **SIZE:** 1–2½". **HABITAT:** On sand in shallow water. **RANGE:** Maryland to Texas.

KELP SCALLOP
Leptopecten latiauratus

LOOK FOR: A small yellowish-brown to rusty scallop with some jagged white lines. Shell is quite thin, with about 12 ribs. **SIZE:** 1". **HABITAT:** On rocks and other hard objects, on kelp, and in sand, all in shallow water. **RANGE:** Central California and southward.

SIZE: 2–3".

HABITAT: Eelgrass beds in shallow water.

RANGE:

59

FLORIDA SPINY JEWEL BOX
Arcinella cornuta

Because most jewel boxes attach one of their shells to an offshore rock—and remain attached even after the mollusk dies— beachcombers rarely find these beautiful bivalves in all their glory. Once in a while both valves are found attached to one another, but usually they break apart before they reach shore. Of the various hard-shelled jewel boxes in the southeastern United States, the distinctive Florida Spiny Jewel Box is probably the one most commonly found on beaches.

Look for: A thick, strongly curved jewel box with small knobs in the spaces between 7–9 rows of spines. White outside, pinkish inside.

Size: 1½–2".

Habitat: Attached to a rock or shell in shallow water.

Range:

LEAFY JEWEL BOX
Chama macerophylla

Look for: An oval to round jewel box covered with rows of leafy frills. Outside may be white, yellow, orange, or purple. **Size:** 1–3". **Habitat:** Attached by left valve to a hard surface in shallow to deep water. **Range:** North Carolina to Texas.

ATLANTIC THORNY OYSTER
Spondylus americanus

Look for: A thick, heavy bivalve with flattened spines up to 3" long. Often whitish, but may be purple, red, or yellow. Badly worn left valve sometimes washes up on beaches. **Size:** 4–5". **Habitat:** Attached by right valve to rocks or coral in shallow to fairly deep water. **Range:** North Carolina to Florida; Texas.

61

NUTTALL'S COCKLE
Clinocardium nuttallii

Cockles are known by shell collectors for their hard, heart-shaped shells decorated with radiating ribs. Many cockles, including Nuttall's Cockle, are taller than they are wide. Cockles use their strong foot to burrow into the sand and to propel themselves across it. Nuttall's Cockle, common along much of the Pacific Coast, is also popularly known as the Basket Cockle.

LOOK FOR: A round whitish cockle, sometimes with dark bands. Valves are higher than wide, with 33–38 squarish ribs and a brown skin.

SIZE: 3–5".

HABITAT: Buried in sand in shallow water.

RANGE:

YELLOW PRICKLY COCKLE
Trachycardium muricatum

LOOK FOR: A smallish, nearly round cockle that has 30–40 ribs covered with sharp scales, especially along valve edges; center of valves may be quite smooth. Creamy white to yellow outside; white inside. **SIZE:** 2". **HABITAT:** In sand in fairly shallow water. **RANGE:** North Carolina to Florida; Texas.

ATLANTIC GIANT COCKLE
Dinocardium robustum

LOOK FOR: A very large, smooth cockle with 32–36 flattish ribs. Tan with reddish-brown patches outside; pinkish inside. Shell is taller than wide. **SIZE:** 3–5". **HABITAT:** In sand in shallow to fairly shallow water. **RANGE:** Virginia to northern Florida; Texas.

NORTHERN QUAHOG
Mercenaria mercenaria

Hard-shelled clams, also known as venus clams, are often round to oval and may be very plain or highly decorated with ridges and colorful lines and rays. The Northern Quahog is most colorful on the inside: white with a purple border. In times past, the shells of Northern Quahogs, especially the purple parts, were prized by Native Americans.

Look for: A thick, heavy, roundish venus clam, off-white with many growth lines. Smooth and white inside, usually with a bright purple rim.

Size: 3–5".

Habitat: In sand or mud in shallow water.

Range:

Sunray Venus
Macrocallista nimbosa

Look for: A large, shiny, very handsome venus clam. Pinkish-gray outside, with darker rays radiating from the beak; inside is smooth and polished, silvery to pinkish. **Size:** 5–6". **Habitat:** Sandy bottoms in shallow water. **Range:** North Carolina to Texas.

Atlantic Surf Clam
Spisula solidissima

Look for: A large creamy-white bivalve with a thin yellowish-brown skin. Shaped like a rounded triangle; smooth outside and in. Often abundant on beaches after storms. **Size:** 5–7". **Habitat:** Sandy bottoms from shoreline to fairly deep water. **Range:** Nova Scotia to South Carolina.

65

PISMO CLAM
Tivela stultorum

Pismo Clams are often dug up from shallow sand by Sea Otters, which may hang around a good bed for days and eat the clams one after another. When you find one of these large, triangular shells on a beach, remember that a Sea Otter may have helped add to your collection.

LOOK FOR: A large venus clam shaped like a rounded triangle. Light gray with brown radiating rays outside and a thin, shiny, light brown skin; white and polished inside.

SIZE: 3–5".

HABITAT: Sandy bottoms in intertidal zone.

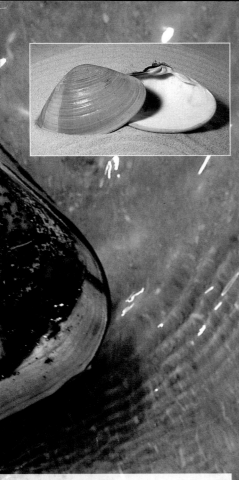

PACIFIC LITTLENECK
Prototheca staminea

LOOK FOR: A roundish, thick-shelled venus clam with many radiating ribs and strong growth lines. Outside may be white to dark brown with many darker patches or none at all; inside is smooth, white to purple. **SIZE:** 2". **HABITAT:** Sandy or muddy bottoms in shallow water. **RANGE:** Alaska to California.

CALIFORNIA BUTTERCLAM
Saxidomus nuttalli

LOOK FOR: A large, oval, brown-gray venus clam with many concentric ridges on the outside. Smooth with a purple stain inside. **SIZE** 3–5". **HABITAT:** Sandy or muddy bottoms in shallow to fairly deep water. **RANGE:** California.

RANGE:

67

VARIABLE COQUINA
Donax variabilis

There are few things as beautiful as a collection of Coquinas, lovely little "butterfly shells" that come in a fabulous variety of colors in stripes, bands, and solids. Coquinas are tide-followers: Upon rising tides, they ride the waves up the beach; when the tide goes out, they move back into deeper water. This is not just mindless surfing: By following the tides in this way, they keep themselves in the part of the surf where food is most abundant. Variable Coquinas can be extremely common on some southern shores.

Look for: A small, colorful, wedge-shaped coquina with bands or rays of darker colors. Inside is smooth, often purplish.

Size: ½–¾".

Habitat: Sandy bottoms in shallow water.

Range:

Alternate Tellin
Tellina alternata

Look for: A flat, oval bivalve with numerous fine growth lines. Usually whitish outside, but may be light pink or yellow; white inside. **Size:** 2–3". **Habitat:** Buried in sand in shallow water. **Range:** North Carolina to Texas.

Rose Petal Tellin
Tellina lineata

Look for: A smooth, delicate, oval bivalve, rosy pink outside and in. Left valve is slightly more inflated than right. Commonly washed ashore. **Size:** 1". **Habitat:** In sand from low-tide line to water 60' deep. **Range:** Florida to Texas.

PACIFIC RAZOR CLAM
Siliqua patula

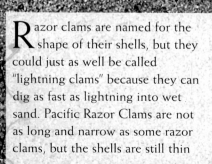

Razor clams are named for the shape of their shells, but they could just as well be called "lightning clams" because they can dig as fast as lightning into wet sand. Pacific Razor Clams are not as long and narrow as some razor clams, but the shells are still thin and sharp enough to slice quickly through sand.

Look for: An oval, thin-shelled razor clam with an olive-green skin. White inside with purple highlights and a prominent rib below the hinge.

Size: 5–6".

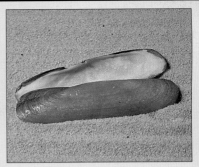

CALIFORNIA TAGELUS
Tagelus californianus

LOOK FOR: A long, narrow, thin-shelled razor clam with fine growth lines and a yellowish skin. White inside. **SIZE:** 2–4". **HABITAT:** Sandy mudflats near low-tide line. **RANGE:** California.

HABITAT: Sand- and mudflats in the intertidal zone.
RANGE:

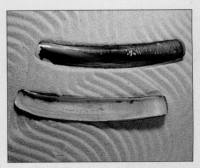

ATLANTIC JACKKNIFE CLAM
Ensis directus

LOOK FOR: An extremely long, narrow, thin-shelled razor clam with squared-off ends. About 6 times as long as wide. Olive-brown skin; white inside. **SIZE:** 5–8". **HABITAT:** Sandy or muddy bottoms in shallow water. **RANGE:** Labrador to South Carolina.

71

PACIFIC GEODUCK
Panopea abrupta

Clams can live as far below the surface of mud and sand as their siphons reach. Geoducks (pronounced GOOEY-ducks) have huge siphons, two to four feet long, that allow them to live deep in the mud. Geoducks and many other clams squirt water from their siphons when they pull them back into their shells, a sort of signpost to their location down below. Weighing as much as eight pounds, the Pacific Geoduck is the largest North American bivalve.

Look for: A huge off-white clam with numerous wavy growth lines. Valves are rounded on one end, flattish and widely gaping on the other, with a weak hinge.

Size: 6–9".

Habitat: Buried deep in mud in shallow water.

Range:

Soft-shelled Clam
Mya arenaria

Look for: An oval clam with gaping valves. Rough, chalky white outside; smooth and white inside, with a spoon-shaped dip at the hinge. **Size:** 3–6". **Habitat:** Buried in mud in shallow water. **Range:** Alaska to San Francisco, California; Labrador to South Carolina.

Pacific Gaper
Tresus nuttallii

Look for: A huge off-white clam with gaping valves. Very similar to the Pacific Geoduck, but more rounded and with a deep, triangular pit at the hinge (visible inside). **Size:** 6–8". **Habitat:** Buried deep in mud in shallow water. **Range:** Alaska to California.

ANGEL WING

Cyrtopleura costata

Like the razor clams, the Angel Wing—a "boring" clam—is an exceptional digger. Boring clams dig by rocking their ridged shells back and forth. You may occasionally find unbroken shells on the beach to add to your collection, but if you want to experience the Angel Wing in its chosen surroundings, you have to get down into the mud and dig. Prepare to get really messy!

LOOK FOR: A beautiful thin, white, wing-shaped boring clam decorated with many scaly ribs. Glistening white inside.

SIZE: 4–7".

HABITAT: Very deep in mud and clay in shallow water.

RANGE:

FLAP-TIP PIDDOCK
Penitella penita

LOOK FOR: A long off-white clam divided into two parts by a groove. Inflated, rounded end has a rough surface; longer, narrower, flatter end is smoother, marked only with growth lines. **SIZE:** 1–2". **HABITAT:** Bored into wood, rocks, cement, and clay from low-tide line to fairly deep water. **RANGE:** Alaska to California.

SHIPWORMS
Teredo species

LOOK FOR: Very small wood-boring clams that have gaping, triangular white valves with winglike projections and sharp edges. Body is long and wormlike. Tunnels are lined with a shelly deposit that the animal leaves behind as it drills its way through wood. **SIZE:** ½". **HABITAT:** In wood in shallow to deep water; on debris ashore and at sea; and in boats. **RANGE:** British Columbia to California; Newfoundland to Florida.

75

ROUNDED PANDORA
Pandora gouldiana

This beautiful pandora rates as one of northeastern North America's loveliest shells, especially when the outer layers are worn down to show the pearly layers underneath. Pandoras are found just below the sandy sea bottom in shallow water, sometimes with the seaweed *Codium* growing from their spouts. Pandoras are often found washed up on beaches with both valves attached.

LOOK FOR: A thin, unusually shaped clam: rounded at both ends with a short spout at the rear through which the siphons protrude. The right valve is flatter than the left. White outside, pearly inside.

SIZE: 1".

HABITAT: Sandy bottoms in shallow water.

RANGE:

COMMON JINGLE SHELL
Anomia simplex

LOOK FOR: A bivalve with two different valves: one thin and curved, usually yellow, silver, or orangy; the other flat and whitish with a hole at the apex. **SIZE:** 1–2". **HABITAT:** Attached to rocks and other shells in shallow water. **RANGE:** Nova Scotia to Texas.

GLASSY LYONSIA
Lyonsia hyalina

LOOK FOR: A small, thin, glassy-looking clam, often with sand grains stuck to the yellowish skin. Shell is rounded at one end, flattened at the other. Shiny and smooth inside. **SIZE:** ½–¾". **HABITAT:** Nestled in sand in shallow to fairly deep water. **RANGE:** Nova Scotia to South Carolina.

RED ABALONE
Haliotis rufescens

The Pacific Coast abalones cling to their rocky homes so tightly that they hardly notice the pounding surf that flows over them. Brave divers swim in strong currents to harvest abalones for their tasty flesh. All abalones have holes along the edge of the shell to inhale and exhale water and to pass waste. The Red Abalone, like its relatives, is most colorful on the inside of its shell, where its iridescence shines beautifully.

LOOK FOR: A large, oval, deep red abalone with 3–4 holes along the edge of the wavy shell. Shimmering pink, pearly, and green inside.

SIZE: 8–12".

BLACK ABALONE
Haliotis cracherodii

LOOK FOR: A smooth, round, black abalone with 5–8 holes along the edge. Inside is silvery with a pink and green sheen. **SIZE:** 5–6". **HABITAT:** On rocks in shallow water. **RANGE:** Oregon to California.

GREEN ABALONE
Haliotis fulgens

LOOK FOR: A round abalone with many spiral ridges and usually 6 holes. Reddish-brown to greenish-brown outside; shimmering blue-green inside. **SIZE:** 6–8". **HABITAT:** On rocks in shallow to fairly deep water. **RANGE:** Monterey, California, and southward.

HABITAT: On rocks in shallow to fairly deep water.

RANGE:

79

The Plate Limpet is one of many rock-loving snails with a hat- or cone-shaped shell. Like abalones, limpets cling to rocks with a foot that fills most of the shell. They wander at night to look for food and usually return to the same neighborhood each day. Plate Limpets are the most common limpets along the northeastern Atlantic coast and can be found quite high up on ocean rocks and in tidepools.

LOOK FOR: A smoothish, oval, light gray limpet mottled and striped with dark brown. Inside has a dark center surrounded by a wide silvery band and a checkered border. Shell is high in calm water, lower in more turbulent water.

SIZE: 1–1½".

HABITAT: Intertidal rocks and tidepools.

RANGE:

RIBBED LIMPET
Lottia digitalis

LOOK FOR: A small, very common limpet with fingerlike ribs and a wavy edge to the shell. Apex is off-center and hooked forward. Dark green-gray with white streaks outside; pearly with brown at center inside. **SIZE:** 1". **HABITAT:** On intertidal rocks. **RANGE:** Alaska to California.

OWL LIMPET
Lottia gigantea

LOOK FOR: A huge, oval limpet. Apex is off-center, near front end. Brown-gray and rough outside; silvery-blue with a wide brown border inside. **SIZE:** 3–4". **HABITAT:** On intertidal rocks near the high-tide line. **RANGE:** California.

Rough Keyhole Limpet
Diodora aspera

If you want to see Rough Keyhole Limpets where they live, get out to the middle and lower tidal zones. Here, where sea stars roam in search of food—including these keyhole limpets—you may find Rough Keyhole Limpets by the dozens. Keyhole limpets cling to rocks like typical limpets but differ in having a hole at their apex.

Look for: A high, oval limpet with a round "keyhole." Outside is grayish with darker bands and numerous beaded ribs; white inside.

Size: 1–2".

Habitat: On rocks in shallow water.

Range:

Volcano Keyhole Limpet
Fissurella volcano
Look for: A high, oval limpet with a keyhole-shaped hole. Outside is pinkish-gray with dark red bands radiating from the apex; white inside. **Size:** 1". **Habitat:** On intertidal rocks. **Range:** California.

Giant Keyhole Limpet
Megathura crenulata
Look for: A very large, low, oval limpet with a large, oval "keyhole" toward the front. Gray to tan outside; in life, the animal's blackish body covers part of its shell. **Size:** 3–5". **Habitat:** On rocks in shallow water. **Range:** Monterey, California, and southward.

PURPLE-RINGED TOP SHELL
Calliostoma annulatum

Because of their neat top-shaped form and fine coloration, top shells are avidly collected everywhere they are found. One of the largest and most magnificent top shells is the Purple-ringed, which lives offshore on rocks and kelp beds. Beachcombers are most likely to find this beautiful shell among the mounds of kelp washed ashore by Pacific breakers.

WESTERN RIBBED TOP SHELL
Calliostoma ligatum

LOOK FOR: A common, thick, broad top shell, nearly as wide as high. Outside is brownish-yellow with lighter spiral cords; worn shells show pearly blue color. **SIZE:** 1". **HABITAT:** Among algae and under rocks in intertidal zone. **RANGE:** Alaska to central California.

BLACK TOP SHELL
Tegula funebralis

LOOK FOR: A smooth, thick top shell with 4–5 somewhat rounded whorls and a black skin covering the pearly surface. **SIZE:** 1–2". **HABITAT:** On intertidal rocks. **RANGE:** British Columbia to California.

LOOK FOR: A steep-sided top shell, yellow with a bright pink band coiling around the shell and beaded cords on each whorl.

SIZE: ¾–1¾".

HABITAT: On rocks and kelp blades.

RANGE:

BLEEDING TOOTH
Nerita peloronta

To see how the Bleeding Tooth got its common name, check out the opening of this colorful rock-loving snail: Its teeth look like they're bleeding. The Bleeding Tooth is one of nine species of nerites that occurs in southern Florida and the Keys. Nerites of many kinds, including the Bleeding Tooth, crowd together in crevices of all sizes.

LOOK FOR: A large, round nerite with 1–2 inner teeth stained bright orange-red. Outside is yellowish-white with red and black zigzag marks.

SIZE: 1–1½".

HABITAT: On rocks in shallow water.

RANGE:

VIRGIN NERITE
Neritina virginea

LOOK FOR: A small nerite. May be light with dark spots, stripes, or wavy lines or dark with light markings, in black, green, cream, tan, and other colors. **SIZE:** ¼–½".
HABITAT: Muddy bottoms in shallow water, including brackish rivers. **RANGE:** Florida to Texas.

EMERALD NERITE
Smaragdia viridis

LOOK FOR: A delicate light to bright green nerite, usually with small white markings. **SIZE:** ¼". **HABITAT:** Attached to eelgrass in shallow water. **RANGE:** Southeastern Florida and Keys; Texas.

It is never a good idea to take animals away from their chosen natural habitats, but if you mistakenly take home a live periwinkle, it has a good chance of surviving until your next trip to the ocean. The Checkered and other periwinkles can close themselves up into their small, thick shells and live in suspended animation for weeks or longer. Checkered Periwinkles usually live far up on shoreline rocks, crowding into crevices.

LOOK FOR: A fairly long, slender periwinkle, red-brown with a white checkered pattern. Apex is sharp and high.

COMMON PERIWINKLE
Littorina littorea

LOOK FOR: A smooth, roundish, brown-black periwinkle. Usually abundant. **SIZE:** ¾–1¼". **HABITAT:** On intertidal rocks. **RANGE:** Labrador to Maryland.

MARSH PERIWINKLE
Littoraria irrorata

LOOK FOR: A pointed, oval periwinkle with spiral ridges. Outside is grayish-white with reddish-brown streaks. **SIZE:** 1". **HABITAT:** On marsh vegetation. **RANGE:** New York to Texas.

SIZE: ½".

HABITAT: On seaweed-covered intertidal rocks.

RANGE:

Angulate Wentletrap
Epitonium angulatum

Wentletraps, usually long, slender, and white, are among the most elegant of shells. The Angulate Wentletrap, commonly found along the driftline of Atlantic Coast beaches, twists like a beautiful miniature spiral staircase. *Wentletrap*, in fact, is Dutch for "spiral staircase." If you look carefully for pure white shells in the beach drift, you will likely add many wentletraps to your collection.

Look for: A perfectly white wentletrap with about 6 whorls, each with 9–10 sharp ribs.

Size: ¾".

HABITAT: Sandy bottoms in shallow water.

RANGE:

BROWN-BANDED WENTLETRAP
Epitonium rupicola

LOOK FOR: A yellowish-white wentletrap with 1–2 brown bands on the larger of the shell's 10 or so whorls. **SIZE:** ½". **HABITAT:** In sand in shallow to fairly deep water. **RANGE:** Cape Cod to Texas.

MANY-RIBBED WENTLETRAP
Epitonium multistriatum

LOOK FOR: A white wentletrap with about 7 whorls. Each whorl has many low, thin ribs. **SIZE:** ½". **HABITAT:** In sand in shallow water. **RANGE:** Cape Cod to Texas.

SCALED WORM SHELL
Serpulorbis squamiger

A t the northern end of its range, the Scaled Worm Shell sometimes lives alone. Farther south, this wormlike mollusk lives in tangled colonies, with many shells intertwined in a large mass. Small marine animals live and hide among the worm shells.

LOOK FOR: A small, tubular, pinkish-white shell that may occur in large, twisted masses or on its own.

SIZE: ½".

HABITAT: On rocks or pilings in shallow water.

RANGE:

WEST INDIAN WORM SHELL
Vermicularia spirata

LOOK FOR: A yellow-brown, ridged worm shell with a sharp, tightly-coiled apex. Young snail resembles screwlike turret shell; shell of mature snail uncoils and stretches out. Some live in tangled masses, others singly. **SIZE:** 4–6". **HABITAT:** Shallow water; often in sponges. **RANGE:** Southeastern Florida and Keys; Texas.

FLORIDA WORM SHELL
Vermicularia knorrii

LOOK FOR: A small yellowish worm shell with clear white whorls at the apex. **SIZE:** 2–3". **HABITAT:** In sponges in shallow water. **RANGE:** North Carolina to Florida; Gulf of Mexico.

DARK CERITH
Cerithium atratum

L ook in a shallow lagoon and watch all the Dark Ceriths and other small shells scurrying around on the ocean floor. Look more closely and you'll see that hermit crabs are the shells' tenants, which is why the shells are moving so quickly. When you collect long, slender ceriths in the shallows, make sure they are empty of living creatures; hermit crabs are very small, so it's easy to overlook them. The Dark Cerith, also known as the Florida Cerith, is common on many Florida beaches.

LOOK FOR: A brownish, sharply pointed cerith with about 10 whorls, beaded ribs, spiral cords, and an oval opening.

CALIFORNIA HORN SNAIL
Cerithidea californica

LOOK FOR: A long, sharply pointed, dark brown horn shell with about 10 whorls, numerous ribs, small spiral cords, and a round opening. **SIZE:** 1–1½". **HABITAT:** Intertidal mudflats. **RANGE:** Central California and southward.

SIZE: 1–1½".

HABITAT: Weedy areas of sandy or rocky bottoms in shallow water.

RANGE:

ALTERNATE BITTIUM
Bittiolum alternatum

LOOK FOR: A very small, pointed, brownish to blackish cerith with 6–8 beaded whorls. Extremely abundant in some areas. **SIZE:** ¼". **HABITAT:** Sandy bottoms from shallow to fairly deep water. **RANGE:** Gulf of St. Lawrence to Virginia.

Some shells are common on beaches, but not the violet snails. The Common Violet Snail and its relatives live out on the open ocean and are cast ashore only after strong winds. On the seas, they blow masses of bubbles and ride them, clinging to the undersides and searching out jellyfish to feed upon. Unlike most other gastropod species, these snails are blind, so they have to happen upon their food by chance.

Look for: A beautiful, fragile, two-toned violet snail; light violet above, dark violet below.

Size: 1–1½".

Habitat: Open ocean.

Range:

Pale Violet Snail
Janthina pallida

Look for: A fragile, rounded violet snail, entirely light violet, with an oval to almost perfectly round opening. **Size:** ½–¾". **Habitat:** Open ocean. **Range:** California; southeastern U.S.

Elongate Violet Snail
Janthina globosa

Look for: A fragile, tall-spired violet snail, medium violet all over, with an opening that is pointed at one end. The most common violet snail on California beaches. **Size:** ¾–1". **Habitat:** Open ocean. **Range:** California; southeastern U.S.

COMMON ATLANTIC SLIPPER SHELL
Crepidula fornicata

Slipper shells resemble not only slippers but also boats, complete with a top deck—a flat shelf that protects the animal's insides. Oyster farmers gather empty slipper shells to spread on the ocean floor so that baby oysters will have something hard to grow on. Live slipper shells, in turn, may grow on top of the oysters, frequently smothering them. The Common Atlantic Slipper Shell is one of the most common beach shells, frequently piling up in masses. Try floating the empty shells upside down in the water.

LOOK FOR: A fairly curved to humpbacked slipper shell, whitish with purplish-brown blotches or radiating lines outside and a flat white platform inside.

SIZE: 1–1½".

HABITAT: Attached to other shells in shallow water.

RANGE:

SPINY SLIPPER SHELL
Crepidula aculeata

LOOK FOR: A white to reddish-brown slipper shell covered with rows of spines. White inner shelf has a ridge down the middle. **SIZE:** ¾–1". **HABITAT:** On rocks and shells in shallow water. **RANGE:** North Carolina to Florida.

SPINY CUP-AND-SAUCER
Crucibulum spinosum

LOOK FOR: A circular, cap-shaped shell with many sharp spines. Yellow to brown with darker brown flecks outside; inside is brown or white stained with brown, and has a white, cuplike shelf. **SIZE:** 1–1½". **HABITAT:** On rocks and shells in fairly shallow water. **RANGE:** Southern California.

QUEEN CONCH
Strombus gigas

Big, heavy, and handsome, conchs are eagerly collected by shell enthusiasts. The Queen Conch has a particularly impressive shell and houses a tasty animal—it may find itself loved right out of existence. This is a protected species in Florida; do not collect it there alive or dead.

The shells of many young conchs, including this one, have thin outer lips; on adults, the lips are thick and flared.

LOOK FOR: A huge conch with a sharp apex; thick, triangular knobs on the whorls; and a wide, flaring lip. Brownish-yellow with a bright pink opening and lip.

FLORIDA FIGHTING CONCH
Strombus alatus

LOOK FOR: A thick yellow-brown conch with darker brown blotches. Knobs may be present on larger whorls. Outer lip is thick, notched at bottom. Dark brown inside. **SIZE:** 3–4". **HABITAT:** Sandy and muddy bottoms in shallow water. **RANGE:** North Carolina to Florida; Texas.

SIZE: 8–12".

HABITAT: Sandy bottoms with eelgrass in shallow water.

RANGE:

HAWKWING CONCH
Strombus raninus

LOOK FOR: A thick yellow-white and dark brown conch. Outer lip is thick and flaring, notched at bottom; inner lip is white, with some pink well inside. **SIZE:** 3–4½". **HABITAT:** Grassy bottoms in shallow water. **RANGE:** Southeastern Florida.

101

LEWIS'S MOON SNAIL
Euspira lewisii

The common clam- and snail-eating moon snails leave their marks—tidy round holes—in their victims' shells after drilling through and sucking out their prey's soft insides. Female moon snails attach their eggs to large "sand collars," circular masses of sand grains stuck together. Beachcombers may find hardened sand collars on sandy beaches. Lewis's Moon Snail, with its baseball-size shell, is the largest living moon snail.

LOOK FOR: A very large, round, yellowish to light brown moon snail with 4–5 whorls; the last whorl, slightly flattened, makes up most of the shell. In life, the animal's fleshy foot nearly covers its shell.

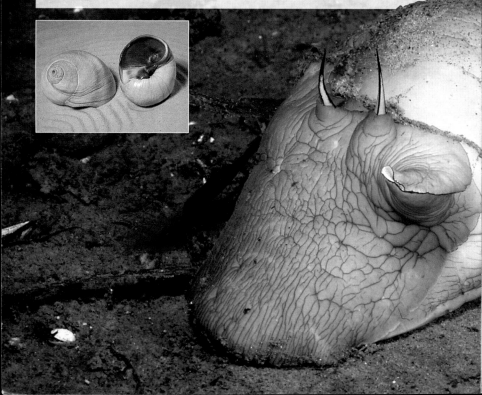

COLORFUL MOON SNAIL
Cypraea canrena

LOOK FOR: A round moon snail, yellowish with dark orange bands and purplish markings. **SIZE:** 1–2". **HABITAT:** Sandy bottoms in shallow to fairly deep water. **RANGE:** North Carolina to Florida; Texas.

WHITE BABY'S EAR
Sinum perspectivum

LOOK FOR: A flat, yellow-white, ear-shaped moon snail with numerous fine spiral lines outside; smooth and pure white inside. **SIZE:** 1–1½". **HABITAT:** Sandy bottoms in shallow water. **RANGE:** Virginia to Texas.

NORTHERN MOON SNAIL
Euspira heros

LOOK FOR: A large, nearly round, blue-gray to white moon snail with evenly rounded whorls. **SIZE:** 3½–5". **HABITAT:** In sand in shallow to deep water. **RANGE:** Gulf of St. Lawrence to North Carolina.

SIZE: 4–5".
HABITAT: Sandy bottoms in shallow water.
RANGE:

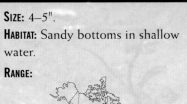

ATLANTIC DEER COWRIE
Macrocypraea cervus

Cowries' shiny oval shells and numerous teeth lining the central opening set these snails apart from other mollusks. In life, a cowrie's capelike mantle covers most of its shell, making it hard to recognize. Most cowries are found in the tropics, but the Atlantic Deer Cowrie, one of the largest in the world, lives in the waters of the southeastern United States. Sometimes reaching seven inches in length, the Atlantic Deer Cowrie is both very beautiful and very large.

LOOK FOR: A large, brown, white-spotted cowrie with a very shiny shell.

SIZE: 3–7".

HABITAT: Under rocks in shallow to fairly deep water.

RANGE:

CHESTNUT COWRIE
Cypraea spadicea

LOOK FOR: A chestnut-colored (reddish-brown) cowrie with a bluish-white edge to the shell; white below. **SIZE:** 1–2½". **HABITAT:** Under rocks and among sea urchins in shallow to deep water. **RANGE:** Monterey, California, and southward.

FLAMINGO TONGUE
Cyphoma gibbosum

LOOK FOR:: A shiny, rectangular, cowrie-like shell, creamy with orange edges. The shell has a ridge across the top and a long, narrow opening. In life, the animal's yellow-orange mantle covers its shell. **SIZE:** 1". **HABITAT:** On sea whips in shallow water. **RANGE:** North Carolina to Florida.

LACE MUREX
Chicoreus dilectus

Rock shells come in a wide variety of shapes and colors, from the elaborate murexes to the drab drills. They live among rocks or corals, feeding on other marine invertebrates by drilling holes into their hard outsides and eating their soft insides. The Lace Murex has everything murex collectors love: a beautiful form, long spines, and fine coloration.

LOOK FOR: A pretty pinkish-white, brownish, or blackish murex with numerous lacy frills and a small, round opening.

SIZE: 2–2½".

APPLE MUREX
Chicoreus pomum

LOOK FOR: A heavy yellowish-white to brown murex with numerous raised ribs and spiral cords, but no long spines. Brown spots on outer lip of opening. **SIZE:** 2–4". **HABITAT:** Oyster beds in shallow water. **RANGE:** North Carolina to Florida; Texas.

WIDE-MOUTHED ROCK SHELL
Plicopurpura patula

LOOK FOR: An oval rock shell with a very large opening. Grayish outside, with spiral rows of knobs. Opening has orangy edges. **SIZE:** 2–3". **HABITAT:** On rocks in shallow water. **RANGE:** Florida. **CAUTION:** Live specimens can permanently stain clothing purple.

HABITAT: On rubble, sand, or mud in shallow water.

RANGE:

ATLANTIC DOGWINKLE
Nucella lapillus

Many northern shells lack the fine colors and sheen of more southerly species. A challenge for northeastern collectors is to find nicely banded Atlantic Dogwinkles, which are typically plainly colored. Look for these shells in rock crevices and under rock overhangs, where their yellowish eggs sometimes hang by the thousands.

LOOK FOR: A common, thick-shelled rock shell. Usually plain white, gray, or yellowish (or orange when young); may be banded with darker color.

SIZE: 1–1½".

ATLANTIC OYSTER DRILL
Urosalpinx cinerea

LOOK FOR: A plain yellow-gray drill with a pointed apex, numerous cords and ribs, and about 5 whorls. Outer lip is sharp. A major predator of oysters. **SIZE:** ¾–1".
HABITAT: Oyster beds in shallow water. **RANGE:** Nova Scotia to Florida; Washington to California.

THICK-LIPPED DRILL
Eupleura caudata

LOOK FOR: A flattish, light gray or brownish drill with numerous ribs. Outer lip is flat. **SIZE:** ¾". **HABITAT:** Oyster beds in shallow water. **RANGE:** Cape Cod to Florida.

HABITAT: On intertidal rocks.

RANGE:

Rock shells are named for where they live: rocky shorelines and ocean bottoms. They also have tough, thick shells that are as hard as rocks. The Giant Forreria is one of North America's largest rock shells, but it doesn't live up to the name "rock shell" very well—it's one of the few of its kind found mostly in sandy areas.

LOOK FOR: A very large yellowish rock shell streaked with brown. Shell has 6–7 whorls with flattened, bladelike ribs and a large white opening.

SIZE: 5–6".

HABITAT: On sand and sandy mud near and on oyster beds in shallow water.

RANGE:

EMARGINATE DOGWINKLE
Nucella emarginata

LOOK FOR: A yellow-brown rock shell with darker spiral bands. The 5 or so whorls have numerous spiral cords. Opening is large and dark red-brown inside. **SIZE:** 1". **HABITAT:** On intertidal rocks. **RANGE:** Alaska to California.

CIRCLED ROCK SNAIL
Ocinebrina circumtexta

LOOK FOR: A grayish-white rock shell with blackish bands. The 4–5 whorls have numerous ribs and deeply cut spiral lines. Teeth on outer lip. **SIZE:** ¾". **HABITAT:** On intertidal rocks. **RANGE:** California.

Lightning Whelk

Busycon sinistrum

The big whelks that wash up on Atlantic beaches are favorites of collectors. One of the loveliest is the distinctive Lightning Whelk. Hold the shell so that the spire is at the top and you can see that the opening is on the left. The Lightning Whelk is one of North America's few large, left-handed shells. Female whelks lay their eggs in nickel-size capsules attached to long strands that sometimes wash ashore. Open the capsules and you may find some tiny, unhatched whelks.

LOOK FOR: A large, left-handed whelk with triangular knobs on the last whorl and a long opening. Young specimens have dark brown markings on an off-white shell; colors fade on older, larger shells.

SIZE: 6–10".

HABITAT: Sandy bottoms in shallow water.

RANGE:

CHANNELED WHELK
Busycotypus canaliculatus

LOOK FOR: A large, pear-shaped whelk with a deep channel (groove) at the upper edge of the last whorl. **SIZE:** 4–7". **HABITAT:** Sand or mud in shallow water. **RANGE:** Cape Cod to northeastern Florida; southern California.

CROWN CONCH
Melongena corona

LOOK FOR: A dark-and-light-banded shell, usually pear-shaped, with 1–2 rows of heavy spines. Sometimes spineless. **SIZE:** 3–4". **HABITAT:** Muddy bottoms in shallow water. **RANGE:** Florida to Alabama.

113

NEW ENGLAND NEPTUNE
Neptunea lyrata decemcostata

The New England Neptune inhabits offshore waters, so to find this handsome shell you must visit beaches after storms. Because the shells are heavy, they often get rolled around in rocks and sand for some time before they are cast ashore, sometimes making perfect specimens a little hard to find.

LOOK FOR: A tan whelk with many brown spiral cords. Often caught in lobster traps.

SIZE: 3½–4".

HABITAT: Rocky bottoms in fairly shallow to deep water.

KELLET'S WHELK
Kelletia kelletii

LOOK FOR: A large, yellowish, thick-shelled whelk with about 7 whorls. 7–9 large, riblike folds per whorl, each fold highest at the center. **SIZE:** 4–5½". **HABITAT:** Rocky and sandy bottoms in shallow to deep water. **RANGE:** California.

WAVED WHELK
Buccinum undatum

LOOK FOR: A yellowish, oval, thick-shelled whelk with broad, wavy ribs. The oval opening has a flared outer lip. **SIZE:** 3½". **HABITAT:** On rocks, sand, or loose gravel. Very abundant from the low-tide line to deep water. **RANGE:** Arctic to New Jersey.

RANGE:

HORSE CONCH
Pleuroploca gigantea

If you chance upon a full-grown Horse Conch, you will be looking at the second-largest gastropod shell on earth and the largest in North America. Only the Australian Trumpet grows larger. Most Horse Conchs found on beaches these days are not record size, but whatever their stature, they are stunning shells. They are also predators, dining mainly on other large gastropods. The Horse Conch grips its prey's trapdoorlike operculum, which prevents the victim from closing itself up.

LOOK FOR: A large orange (young) to orange-brown conch with dark brown, flaking skin; spiral cords; and large, riblike, knobby folds. Spindle-shaped: rounded in the middle and tapering to a point at both ends.

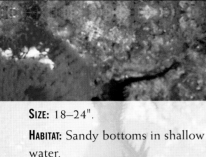

SIZE: 18–24".

HABITAT: Sandy bottoms in shallow water.

RANGE:

TRUE TULIP
Fasciolaria tulipa

LOOK FOR: A shiny, gray-white to orangy, spindle-shaped shell with brownish splotches and fine, dark, spiral lines. **SIZE:** 4–6". **HABITAT:** Sandy bottoms in shallow water. **RANGE:** North Carolina to Texas.

BANDED TULIP
Fasciolaria lilium

LOOK FOR: A tulip shell very similar to the True Tulip but whitish to orange-yellow. The dark spiral lines are not crowded (as in the True Tulip). **SIZE:** 3–4". **HABITAT:** Sandy or muddy bottoms in shallow water. **RANGE:** North Carolina to Texas.

PURPLE DWARF OLIVE
Olivella biplicata

Olives are among the shiniest, smoothest shells on the beach. They are nearly always long and cylindrical, with a long, narrow opening and a small, conical spire. The Purple Dwarf Olive is small but common and brightly colored, and so ends up in many beach strollers' pockets. Look for Purple Dwarf Olives burrowing just below the surface of sandflats.

Look for: A blue-gray olive with purple at the top of each whorl and on the base of the shell. The opening is narrow at the top, wider at the bottom.

Size: 1".

Habitat: Sandy bottoms in shallow to deep water.

Range:

LETTERED OLIVE
Oliva sayana

Look for: A large, shiny, yellowish to tan olive shell with numerous red-brown markings. **Size:** 2–2½". **Habitat:** Sandy bottoms in shallow water. **Range:** South Carolina to Texas.

NETTED OLIVE
Oliva reticularis

Look for: An olive shell very similar to the Lettered Olive, but smaller, more rounded, and lighter in color, with a clearer pattern of dark lines. **Size:** 1–2". **Habitat:** In sand in shallow water. **Range:** Southeastern Florida and Keys.

CALIFORNIA CONE
Conus californicus

Cone shells display a wide array of markings, texture, and coloration, but all share the conical shape for which they are named. The California Cone may not be the flashiest cone in the world, but it is a favorite with Pacific Coast collectors.

LOOK FOR: A yellowish-brown cone with a low, rounded spire and 6–7 whorls. This is the only cone commonly found along the California coast.

SIZE: 1".

HABITAT: Rocky bottoms in shallow water.

RANGE:

CAUTION: Living cones have a tiny, poisonous, harpoonlike tooth for capturing prey; do not handle living specimens.

JASPER CONE
Conus pealii

LOOK FOR: A small white, gray, or tan cone with darker markings. About 10 whorls with many spiral lines cut into shell. **SIZE:** ½–1". **HABITAT:** Sandy bottoms in shallow to fairly deep water. **RANGE:** Southern Florida.

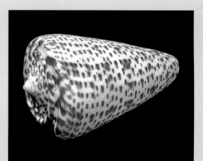

ALPHABET CONE
Conus spurius

LOOK FOR: A rather large, creamy-white cone. May have spiral bands of red-brown splotches, yellowish bands, or other markings, some resembling letters of the alphabet. Top of cone is quite flat; apex is sharply pointed. **SIZE:** 2–3". **HABITAT:** Sandy bottoms in shallow water. **RANGE:** Florida.

CALIFORNIA BUBBLE
Bulla gouldiana

The bubble shells have surprisingly light and fragile shells. After the animal that lives in them dies, the shells can float and ride the waves as far up onto the beach as the surf will carry them. At the highest tide line, you can often find empty bubble shells in perfect condition. At night, live California Bubbles glide over the shallows; during the day, they burrow in mud, just below the surface.

LOOK FOR: A fragile, oval bubble shell, pinkish to brown with many darker markings. Last whorl has a flaring lip and hides other whorls.

SIZE: 1½".

HABITAT: Muddy bottoms in shallow water.

RANGE: .

STRIATE BUBBLE
Bulla striata

LOOK FOR: A light pinkish-brown bubble shell with many dark flecks and a white opening. Common and easily found on southeastern beaches. SIZE: ¾–1". HABITAT: Grassy mudflats in shallow water. RANGE: North Carolina to Texas.

SOLITARY GLASSY BUBBLE
Haminoea solitaria

LOOK FOR: A very fragile white to yellowish bubble shell that has a sunken apex with a delicate lip extending beyond it. SIZE: ¼–½". HABITAT: Sandy bottoms in shallow water. RANGE: Cape Cod to North Carolina.

CARIBBEAN HELMET
Cassis tuberosa

The Caribbean Helmet is the most common of the three helmet shells that live in the southeastern United States. Like its relatives, it plows along shallow, sandy bottoms in search of its favorite foods, sand dollars and sea urchins. All the helmets are highly prized for their shells; collectors love them for their size and beauty, and jewelry makers use them to make cameos.

SCOTCH BONNET
Phalium granulatum

LOOK FOR: A rounded orange-yellow helmet shell with many squarish orange-brown splotches and numerous spiral grooves. White lip of opening has teeth on the outside, grooves on the inside. **SIZE:** 2–4". **HABITAT:** Sandy bottoms in shallow to fairly shallow water. **RANGE:** North Carolina to Florida.

ATLANTIC WOOD LOUSE
Morum oniscus

LOOK FOR: A small, solid, triangular helmet shell with spiral rows of rounded knobs. Teeth on outer lip of whitish opening. **SIZE:** ⅝"–1". **HABITAT:** Coral reefs and coral debris in shallow water. **RANGE:** Florida Keys.

LOOK FOR: A massive helmet shell with a distinctly triangular bottom. Brownish-yellow with many dark blotches above; the dark brown opening has large teeth along the outer lip, smaller folds along the inner lip.

SIZE: 5–7".

HABITAT: Shallow, sandy bottoms.

RANGE:

COMMON FIG SHELL
Ficus communis

On the soft, sandy beaches of Florida's Gulf coast, the wonderfully thin but sturdy shells of the Common Fig wash ashore quite frequently. The sun-bleached specimens found high up in the tide drift are hardly a match for the glossy shells newly tossed up by the sea. Like helmet shells, live figs feed on sea urchins and sand dollars.

Look for: A creamy to light brown, pear-shaped shell decorated with small brownish spots. The surface is etched with small spiral cords and fine growth lines.

Size: 3–4".

Habitat: Sandy bottoms in shallow water.

Range:

ATLANTIC PARTRIDGE TUN
Tonna pennata

Look for: A large, thin, glossy, pear-shaped shell, whitish with numerous brown splotches and spiral ridges. Opening is quite large. Perfect specimens do not often wash ashore. **Size:** 3–5". **Habitat:** Sandy bottoms offshore. **Range:** Southern Florida.

GIANT TUN
Tonna galea

Look for: A very large, round, inflated shell with many strong spiral ridges and a large opening. Resembles the Atlantic Partridge Tun, but is much rounder and can grow much larger. Because the shell is fragile, perfect specimens are hard to find ashore. **Size:** 6–10". **Habitat:** Sandy bottoms offshore. **Range:** North Carolina to Mexico.

127

INDIAN MONEY TUSK SHELL
Antalis pretiosum

Hundreds of species of tusk shells live in marine waters around the world. Indian Money Tusks typically live well away from the coast, so it can take a lot of beachcombing to find their shells. But their curving, tusklike shape is so unusual that the search is worth your while. All tusk shells live partially buried in the sand or mud, with the narrow end sticking up into the water. In times past, Pacific Coast Native Americans strung these shells together and used them for trade, ceremony, and decoration.

LOOK FOR: A smooth, sturdy, white tusk shell.

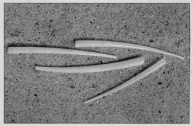

IVORY TUSK SHELL
Graptacme eborea

LOOK FOR: A delicate white, pinkish, or yellowish tusk shell with a very fine slit at the narrow end. **SIZE:** 2". **HABITAT:** Sandy bottoms in shallow water. **RANGE:** North Carolina to Texas.

AMERICAN TUSK SHELL
Dentalium americanum

LOOK FOR: A dull white tusk shell with lengthwise ribs. Shell is six-sided, not rounded like most other tusk shells. **SIZE:** ¾–1¼". **HABITAT:** Sandy and clay bottoms in fairly deep to deep water. **RANGE:** North Carolina to Texas.

SIZE: 1½–2".

HABITAT: Sandy or muddy bottoms in fairly shallow to fairly deep water.

RANGE:

WEST INDIAN GREEN CHITON
Chiton tuberculatus

This big, beautiful chiton is one of several found in Florida. During the day, chitons cling extremely tightly to rocks on jetties and seawalls. Don't try to pry chitons off rocks—doing so can easily hurt or even kill these animals. At night, they loosen their grip and creep around in search of food, mainly algae.

When chitons die, they soon fall apart, so perhaps the best way to add chiton shells to your collection is by taking a photograph or drawing a picture.

LOOK FOR: A large chiton with brown, greenish, gray, or blackish valves that have fine ribs. The girdle resembles snakeskin, with alternating lighter and darker areas.

EASTERN BEADED CHITON
Chaetopleura apiculata

LOOK FOR: A small, plain, gray-brown chiton with many tiny beads on the valves. The most common chiton along much of the Atlantic Coast. **SIZE:** ½–¾". **HABITAT:** On and under rocks in shallow to fairly deep water. **RANGE:** Massachusetts to both coasts of Florida; Texas.

NORTHERN RED CHITON
Tonicella rubra

LOOK FOR: A small, rather narrow, light red chiton with darker blotches. Frequently found attached to kelp roots that have washed ashore. **SIZE:** ½–¾". **HABITAT:** On rocks and seaweed roots in shallow to deep water. **RANGE:** Alaska to California; Arctic to Connecticut.

LINED RED CHITON
Tonicella lineata

Of all the chitons on the Pacific Coast, the Lined Red Chiton is certainly one of the most striking. The bright, wavy lines covering the shell make this species stand out on its rocky home. Lined Red Chitons feed on colorful coral-like algae, and you can search for them anywhere such algae grows on coastal rocks.

LOOK FOR: An oval, orange to purple chiton that has wavy reddish and white lines and a smooth girdle with alternating brown and gray areas.

SIZE: 1½".

Habitat: On rocks in shallow water.
Range:

GIANT PACIFIC CHITON
Cryptochiton stelleri

Look for: An enormous chiton that looks like a deflated football stuck to the rocks. The leathery yellow-brown to red-brown girdle completely covers the white valves. **Size:** 8–14". **Habitat:** On intertidal rocks. **Range:** Alaska to California.

BLACK KATY CHITON
Katharina tunicata

Look for: A long, oval chiton with bluish-white valves mostly covered by the very large, shiny, black girdle. **Size:** 3". **Habitat:** On intertidal rocks. **Range:** Alaska to California.

133

GREATER ARGONAUT
Argonauta argo

Argonauts are ocean-dwelling mollusks related to octopuses. Two of the tentacle arms of the female argonaut are broad and flat and release a substance that dries into the famous argonaut "shell." The shell is actually a case in which the female lays her eggs. During and after storms, these cases sometimes wash ashore.

LOOK FOR: A fragile, white, spiral shell with numerous narrow, riblike folds. The keel, or narrow edge, is brownish and knobby.

SIZE: 6–8".

HABITAT: Open ocean.

RANGE:

WINGED ARGONAUT
Argonauta hians

LOOK FOR: A fragile, brown, spiral shell with many wavy folds. **SIZE:** 2–3". **HABITAT:** Warm open ocean waters. **RANGE:** Southern California and Florida.

RAM'S HORN
Spirula spirula

LOOK FOR: A thin, white, loosely coiled shell; resembles a miniature ram's horn. This is the internal shell of the Common Spirula, a squidlike mollusk that lives in deep water. After the animal dies, its shell floats to the surface and eventually washes ashore. **SIZE:** 1". **HABITAT:** Open ocean. **RANGE:** Massachusetts to Texas.

135

EASTERN FLOATER MUSSEL
Pyganodon cataracta

This large, thin-shelled clam washes up along the edges of ponds and lakes. Muskrats feast on freshwater mussels and will leave small piles of shells after eating the mollusks' tasty insides. The fragile shells of Eastern Floater Mussels serve the living mollusk well, but they tend to dry up and crack in shell collections.

Look for: A large, fragile, yellow-brown to greenish mussel with a flattened ridge at the rear. Pearly inside.

Size: 5–6".

Habitat: Mainly in mud, but also in

EASTERN ELLIPTIO MUSSEL
Elliptio complanata

LOOK FOR: A thin, oval, greenish-brown to black mussel. Smooth and dull outside, sometimes with faint color and rays; tinged with purple inside. **SIZE:** 3–5". **HABITAT:** In mud or sand of lakes and ponds. **RANGE:** Gulf of St. Lawrence to Georgia.

THREERIDGE MUSSEL
Amblema plicata

LOOK FOR: A large, heavy, thick shell, rounded to oval at one end, squarish at the other, with 3–4 ridges. Brownish-green (young shells) or blackish (older shells) outside; pearly white inside. **SIZE:** 4–7". **HABITAT:** In mud, sand, or gravel in small to large rivers. **RANGE:** Saskatchewan; Great Lakes region; central and southeastern U.S.

sand and gravel, of rivers, lakes, and ponds.

RANGE:

137

FINGERNAIL CLAMS
Sphaerium species

D own in the muck at the bottom of ponds and slow-moving streams live the tiny fingernail clams. Get out a strainer or reach down to the base of the Pickerelweeds and cattails and pull up a handful of the gunk that fingernail clams call home. You should be able to find an empty shell for your collection.

LOOK FOR: A very small, thin-shelled, round to oval clam. Some shells have strong growth lines, others are nearly smooth. Yellowish to brown outside.

SIZE: $1/4"-1/2"$.

HABITAT: Muddy and sandy bottoms in lakes, ponds, and streams.

RANGE:

ZEBRA MUSSEL
Dreissena polymorpha

LOOK FOR: A teardrop-shaped mussel, yellowish-tan to dark brown with rows of wavy bands outside; bluish-white inside. **SIZE:** 1". **HABITAT:** Attached to solid objects, often in large clumps, in rivers, lakes, and streams. **RANGE:** Central U.S. east to Vermont and southeast to Georgia.

ASIAN CLAM
Corbicula fluminea

LOOK FOR: A solid, rounded to triangular clam with many parallel ridges and tiny hinge teeth. Yellow-brown with a black skin. Apex is usually worn down. **SIZE:** $1-2½"$. **HABITAT:** In sand, silt, or mud of ponds, lakes, and rivers. **RANGE:**: Widespread in U.S.

SWAMP POND SNAIL
Lymnaea stagnalis

These big brown snails prefer quiet, weedy waters to fast-moving currents and often can be found clinging to the undersides of water plants. They need air to breathe, however, and so make periodic trips to the surface.

LOOK FOR: A large, brown, thin-shelled snail with a narrow, pointed apex and a rounded body whorl.

SIZE: 2–2¼".

HABITAT: On any surface in ponds and slow-moving streams.

RANGE:

TADPOLE SNAILS
Physa species

LOOK FOR: A smooth, small to medium-size, left-handed snail with a pointed spire. Shell is often thin, with a large opening. **SIZE:** ¼–1". **HABITAT:** In almost all fresh waters. Often abundant in mildly polluted waters. **RANGE:** All North America.

MARSH RAM'S HORN
Planorbella trivolvis

LOOK FOR: A flat reddish-brown to light yellow snail with about 3 whorls. **SIZE:** ½–1". **HABITAT:** On rocks and branches in lakes, ponds, and slow-moving streams. **RANGE:** Canada and northern U.S.

FLORIDA APPLE SNAIL
Pomacea paludosa

The big, colorful empty shells of Florida Apple Snails are easy to find in regions where they live. Of course, Snail Kites and Limpkins, two birds that specialize in eating Florida Apple Snails, want to find the snails alive. Snail Kites have a hooked bill that curves into the snail's opening and lifts out the mollusk meat inside.

CHINESE MYSTERY SNAIL
Cipangopaludina chinensis

LOOK FOR: A large, smooth, yellow-brown to green-brown snail with a thin brown operculum. Rounded shell has 5–6 whorls. Species of mystery snails are difficult to tell apart, earning them their name. **SIZE:** 2–2½". **HABITAT:** On mud of ponds and lakes, especially in urban areas. **RANGE:** Southern Canada and eastern U.S.

LOOK FOR: A large, smooth, rounded snail with a very large, rounded opening covered by a trapdoorlike operculum. The very large last whorl makes up most of the shell. Light green or brown with darker spiral bands.

SIZE: 2–2½".

HABITAT: On marsh vegetation in ponds and slow-moving water.

RANGE:

BROWN MYSTERY SNAIL
Campeloma decisum

LOOK FOR: A large, pointed, yellowish to brown snail with an ear-shaped operculum. **SIZE:** 1½–2". **HABITAT:** On muddy or muddy-sandy bottoms in lakes and slow-moving waters. **RANGE:** East coast of North America.

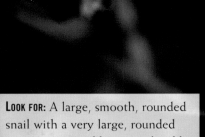

FLORIDA TREE SNAIL
Liguus fasciatus

The wonderfully colored Florida Tree Snail may be the most beautiful land snail in the world, with more than 50 known color variations. Overcollecting and the loss of suitable habitat in the Everglades and other areas of southern Florida have made the Florida Tree Snail hard to find in these places.

Look for: A large tree snail with fine spiral bands, large blotches of color, and other decorations. The shell is long, with 4–5 whorls, a pointed apex, and a rounded opening.

Size: 2".

Habitat: On lichen-covered trees.

Range:

White-lipped Snail
Neohelix albolabris

Look for: A large, light brown woodland snail with a white lip on the toothless opening and a high, rounded shell. Animal is cream-colored with a dark head. **Size:** 1–1¼". **Habitat:** On the ground in broadleaf woodlands. **Range:** Southeastern Canada and eastern U.S.

Rosy Wolfsnail
Euglandina rosea

Look for: A long, narrow snail with many fine, lengthwise lines and a pink opening (color fades with age). Feeds on other snails. **Size:** 2–2½". **Habitat:** Under stones in damp areas of woodlands and gardens. **Range:** North Carolina to Florida.

145

AMBER SNAILS
Succinea species

There are many species of amber snails, and most look so much alike that it takes an expert to tell one from another. You may not be able to tell which species is which, but amber snails' thin, almost see-through shells and huge body whorls set them apart from other snails.

LOOK FOR: A fragile amber-colored snail with 3–4 whorls, the last one very large; a large, oval opening; and a sharp outer lip.

SIZE: ¼–1".

HABITAT: On vegetation or wet soil at the edges of ponds, streams, and marshes.

FOREST DISK SNAIL
Discus whitneyi

LOOK FOR: A tiny, light brown snail shell with 3–4 whorls and numerous ridges. **SIZE:** ¼". **HABITAT:** Fields and woodland edges. **RANGE:** Western and northern U.S.

BANDED TIGER SNAIL
Anguispira kochi

LOOK FOR: A smooth yellow to light brown snail with 1–2 reddish-brown spiral bands and about 6 whorls. **SIZE:** ½–1". **HABITAT:** Under logs near heavily wooded ravines or large rivers. **RANGE:** Washington and Oregon east to Pennsylvania and Kentucky.

RANGE:

GROVE SNAIL
Cepaea nemoralis

Grove Snails gnaw away down on the lowest leaves of garden plants or out on the highest pods of wild milkweeds. A group of Grove Snails in a single meadow or garden will display quite a range in shell decoration, with varying numbers of wide and narrow spiral lines. One of the prettiest land snails in North America, the Grove Snail is an import from central and western Europe.

LOOK FOR: A pinkish-tan or yellow snail with 1 or a few dark spiral lines, a nearly clear shell, and a brown lip on the opening.

SIZE: ¾–1".

HABITAT: Gardens and fields.

RANGE:

CELLAR GLASS SNAIL
Oxychilus cellarius

LOOK FOR: A fairly flat, shiny, almost transparent snail, whitish to very light yellow. **SIZE:** ¼". **HABITAT:** In towns, under rocks and boards, in cellars, and often in greenhouses. **RANGE:** All North America.

BROWN GARDEN SNAIL
Helix aspersa

LOOK FOR: A rounded, light brown snail with darker blotchy bands. A major pest in gardens, where it eats both leaves and flowers. Originally imported to U.S. as a food item. **SIZE:** 1½". **HABITAT:** Gardens and moist places, often near towns. **RANGE:** Widespread in southern U.S.

How to use the reference section

Chestnut Cowries page 105

The **Glossary,** which begins below, contains terms used by malacologists and naturalists. If you run across a word in this book that you do not understand, check the glossary for a definition. Also in this section is a list of **Resources,** including books, videos, organizations, and Web sites devoted to North American shells, as well as a table for learning how to convert measurements to metrics. Finally, there is an **Index** of all the species covered in the field guide section of this book.

GLOSSARY

Algae
Simple plants that grow in water, such as seaweeds and pond scum.

Apex
The tip or high point of a shell.

Beak
The earliest-formed part of a bivalve shell, usually right above the hinge.

Body whorl
The last and usually largest whorl (coil) in a gastropod's shell.

Brackish
Describes a mixture of salt and fresh water.

Camouflage
Colors or patterns on an animal that help it blend in with its environment.

Concentric
Sharing a center. In bivalves, describes lines or ridges that form a pattern similar to the arching bands of color in a rainbow.

Conchologist
A person who studies the shells of mollusks.

Cords
In gastropods, narrow, rounded ridges that coil around the shell.

Eelgrass
A water plant with long, limp leaves.

Freshwater
A body of water that is not salty, such as a river, pond, lake, or stream.

Gaping
In bivalves, describes valves that do not close completely.

Girdle
The band of tissue that holds the pieces of a chiton's shell together.

Growth lines
Lines on a shell that mark stages of its growth.

Habitat
The environment in which an animal lives.

High-tide line
The highest point on the shore that the ocean reaches each day.

Hinge
The connection between a bivalve's two shells that allows them to open and close.

Intertidal zone
The area of the shore between the highest and lowest points that the tides reach each day.

Invertebrate
An animal without a backbone.

Kelp
Seaweed with long, leaflike blades.

Knob
A rounded bump or projection on a shell.

Larva (plural: larvae)
A stage of growth before an animal reaches its mature form.

Left-handed
Describes a gastropod shell in which the opening is on the left side when the shell is held upright.

Lichen
A plantlike growth on a hard surface, such as a rock.

Lip
The edge of the opening in a gastropod's shell.

Low-tide line
The lowest point on the shore that the ocean retreats to when the tide goes out each day.

Malacologist
A person who studies mollusks.

Mantle
A special organ that mollusks use to make their shells.

Marine
Saltwater or ocean.

Mollusk
A soft-bodied invertebrate that usually has a protective shell.

Operculum
A trapdoorlike body part that a mollusk can close over its shell opening.

Pearl
A bead that forms in a mollusk when a foreign particle gets inside its shell.

Predator
An animal that hunts and kills other animals for food.

Prey
An animal caught by predators for food.

Radiating
Describes ribs or rays of color that fan out from the beak of a bivalve shell.

Range
The geographic area where a species normally lives.

Ribs
Raised lines that radiate on a bivalve shell and run lengthwise on a gastropod shell.

Ridges
Raised lines that run across a bivalve shell and coil around a gastropod shell.

Sea whip
A long, whiplike soft coral.

Sediment
Materials such as sand and mud that settle at the bottom of a body of water.

Siphon
A tube through which bivalves eat, breathe, and release waste.

Skin
A thin outer covering found on some shells.

Species
Animals that look alike and can mate to produce young.

Spines
Pointed projections on a shell.

Spiral
A coiled shape or pattern.

Spire
The upper whorls (coils) of a gastropod shell, ending in the apex.

Tentacle
A flexible growth on a mollusk or other invertebrate, used for feeling or grasping.

Valve
Shell.

Vegetation
Plant life.

Vertebrate
An animal with a backbone.

Whorl
A turn or twist in a gastropod's coiled shell.

A shell-strewn Florida beach

FOR FURTHER READING

The American Museum of Natural History Guide to Shells: Land, Freshwater, and Marine from Nova Scotia to Florida
Emerson and Jacobson
Alfred A. Knopf, 1976

Discovering Seashells
Douglas Florian
Scribner, 1986

The Encyclopedia of Shells
Kenneth Wye
Knickerbocker Press, 1998

Eyewitness Explorer Series: Shells
Jennifer Coldrey
DK Publishing, 1993

Eyewitness Series: Shell
Alex Arthur
Alfred A. Knopf, 1989

A Guide to Field Identification: Seashells of North America
R. Tucker Abbott
Golden Books, 1986

National Audubon Society Field Guide to North American Seashells
Harald A. Rehder
Alfred A. Knopf, 1997

National Audubon Society Field Guide to North American Seashore Creatures
Norman A. Meinkoth
Alfred A. Knopf, 1995

National Audubon Society Pocket Guide: Familiar Seashells of North America
Harald A. Rehder
Alfred A. Knopf, 1998

Seashells in My Pocket: A Child's Guide to Exploring the Atlantic Coast from Maine to North Carolina
Judith Hansen
Appalachian Mountain Club Books, 1988

VIDEO

Shell (Eyewitness Video)
Dorling Kindersley Vision

ORGANIZATIONS

American Malacological Society, Inc.
c/o Eugene P. Keferl
Department of Natural Sciences & Mathematics
Coastal Georgia Community College
3700 Altama Ave.
Brunswick, GA 31520-3644
http://erato.acnatsci.org/ams

Conchologists of America
c/o Lynn Scheu
1222 Holsworth Lane
Louisville, KY 40222-6616
(502) 423-0469
http://coa.acnatsci.org/conch net

National Audubon Society
Earth Stewards Campaign
700 Broadway
New York, NY 10003-9562
http://www.audubon.org/campaign/refuge/earthstewards.html

National Wildlife Federation
Earthsavers, Dept. HH
8925 Leesburg Pike
Vienna, VA 22184
(703) 790-4000
http://www.nwf.org/nwf/kids

The Nature Conservancy
International Headquarters
1815 North Lynn Street
Arlington, VA 22209
Tel: 703-841-5300
http://www.tnc.org

WEB SITES

American Museum of Natural History: Online Field Journal for Children:
http://www.amnh.org/ncslet/online_field_journal

Audubon's "Educate Yourself" Web Site:
http://www.audubon.org/educate

Conchologists of America: Conch-Net: Kid's Section:
http://coa.acnatsci.org/conchnet/fun.htm

Conchology:
http://www.conchology.uunethost.be

Jacksonville Shell Club:
http://home.sprynet.com/~wfrank/jacksonv.htm

Monterey Bay Aquarium E-quarium:
http://www.mbayaq.org

National Geographic Society: Kids' Page:
http://www.nationalgeographic.com/kids

National Shellfisheries Organization:
http://www.shellfish.org

National Wildlife Federation: Kids' Page:
http://www.nwf.org/nwf/kids

On-line Nature Guide:
http://www.eNature.com

Seashell Identification Guide:
www.seashells.org/identcatagories/mollusksmntonc.htm

Red Abalone page 78

Make it metric

Here is a chart you can use to change measurements of size, distance, weight, and temperature to their metric equivalents.

	multiply by
inches to millimeters	25
inches to centimeters	2.5
feet to meters	0.3
yards to meters	0.9
miles to kilometers	1.6
square miles to square kilometers	2.6
ounces to grams	28.3
pounds to kilograms	.45
Fahrenheit to Centigrade	subtract 32 and multiply by .55

Page numbers in **bold type** point to a shell's page in the field guide.

White-lipped Snail
page 145

Greater Argonaut page 134

Clam shell on an Alaska beach

PHOTO CREDITS

Credits are listed by page,
from left to right, top to bottom.

87b: Kjell B. Sandved
87c (inset): David B. Snyder
88a: Andrew J. Martinez
88b (inset): Kjell B. Sandved
89a: Frederick D. Atwood
89b: Bill Beatty
90: Andrew J. Martinez
91a: Andrew J. Martinez
91b: Charlotte M. Lloyd
92: Conlin/Innerspace Visions
93a: Frederick D. Atwood
93b: Frederick D. Atwood
93c (inset): Charlotte M. Lloyd
94: Andrew J. Martinez
95a: Kjell B. Sandved
95b: Charlotte M. Lloyd
96: Robert Hermes/Photo
  Researchers, Inc.
97a: Charlotte M. Lloyd
97b: Charlotte M. Lloyd
97c (inset): Kathy Adams Clark/
  KAC Productions
98a: Andrew J. Martinez
98b (inset): Frederick D. Atwood
99a: Charlotte M. Lloyd
99b: Charlotte M. Lloyd
100: Andrew J. Martinez
101a (inset): Ronald N. Wilson
101b: Ronald N. Wilson
101c: Frederick D. Atwood
102a: Andrew J. Martinez
102b (inset): Kjell B. Sandved
103a: Charlotte M. Lloyd
103b: Charlotte M. Lloyd
103c: Kjell B. Sandved
104: Doug Perrine/Innerspace Visions
105a: Richard Herrmann
105b (inset): Ronald N. Wilson
105c: Frederick D. Atwood
106: Andrew J. Martinez
107a (inset): Charlotte M. Lloyd
107b: Ronald N. Wilson
107c: Charlotte M. Lloyd
108: Gary Meszaros/Visuals Unlimited
109a: E. R. Degginger/Bruce Coleman,
  Inc.
109b: Kjell B. Sandved
110: Andrew J. Martinez
111a: Kjell B. Sandved
111b: Kjell B. Sandved
112: Jen & Des Bartlett/Bruce
  Coleman, Inc.
113a: Andrew J. Martinez
113b (inset): Frederick D. Atwood
113c: Kjell B. Sandved
114: Andrew J. Martinez
115a (inset): Andrew J. Martinez
115b: David Wrobel/Innerspace Visions
115c: Kjell B. Sandved
116a: E. R. Degginger/Bruce
  Coleman, Inc.
116b (inset): J. H. Carmichael, Jr./Bruce
  Coleman, Inc.
117a: David B. Snyder
117b: Frederick D. Atwood
118a: Kaj R. Svensson/SPL/Photo
  Researchers, Inc.

118b (inset): Kjell B. Sandved
119a: Frederick D. Atwood
119b: Andrew J. Martinez
120: David Wrobel/Innerspace Visions
121a: Department of Invertebrates,
  American Museum of Natural History
121b: E. R. Degginger/Bruce
  Coleman, Inc.
121c (inset): Kjell B. Sandved
122: Richard Herrmann
123a: Frederick D. Atwood
123b (inset): E. R. Degginger/Bruce
  Coleman, Inc.
123c: Charlotte M. Lloyd
124a: Nancy Sefton/Photo
  Researchers, Inc.
125a: Charlotte M. Lloyd
125b: Charlotte M. Lloyd
125c (inset): Frederick D. Atwood
126: Chesher/Photo Researchers, Inc.
127a: Charlotte M. Lloyd
127b: Charlotte M. Lloyd
127c (inset): Frederick D. Atwood
128: Charlotte M. Lloyd
129a: Charlotte M. Lloyd
129b: Charlotte M. Lloyd
130: Andrew J. Martinez
131a: Norman A. Meinkoth
131b: Gustav W. Verderber/Visuals
  Unlimited
132: Conlin/Innerspace Visions
133a: Kevin & Betty Collins/Visuals
  Unlimited
133b: Gerald & Buff Corsi/Visuals
  Unlimited
133c (inset): Kerry T. Givens/Bruce
  Coleman, Inc.
134: Norbert Wu
135a: Charlotte M. Lloyd
135b (inset): Department of
  Invertebrates, American Museum of
  Natural History
135c: Kerry T. Givens/Bruce Coleman,
  Inc.
136: Department of Invertebrates,
  American Museum of Natural History
137a: Charlotte M. Lloyd
137b: Richard Thom/Visuals Unlimited
138: Department of Invertebrates,
  American Museum of Natural History
139a: Herb Segars
139b: Charlotte M. Lloyd
140: Ken Brate/Photo Researchers, Inc.
141a: Department of Invertebrates,
  American Museum of Natural History
141b: Frederick D. Atwood
142: James R. Fisher/Photo
  Researchers, Inc.
143a: Charlotte M. Lloyd
143b: Charlotte M. Lloyd
143c (inset): Frederick D. Atwood
144: Gary Meszaros/Visuals Unlimited
145a: Rob & Ann Simpson
145b: Treat Davidson/Photo
  Researchers, Inc.
145c (inset): J. H. Carmichael, Jr./Bruce
  Coleman, Inc.

146: Frank Hecker/OKAPIA/Photo
  Researchers, Inc.
147a: Charlotte M. Lloyd
147b: L. West/Bruce Coleman, Inc.
148: Rob & Ann Simpson
149a: Charlotte M. Lloyd
149b: Frederick D. Atwood
150–151: Wendell Metzen/Bruce
  Coleman, Inc.
150a: Wayne & Karen Brown/Brown &
  Company Photography
152: Richard Howard
153: Frank S. Balthis
154–155: Charles R. Belinky/Photo
  Researchers, Inc.
156: Norbert Wu
157: Don Cornelius

*Photo Researchers, Inc.
60 East 56th Street
New York, NY 10022

Prepared and produced by
Chanticleer Press, Inc.

Publisher: Andrew Stewart
Founder: Paul Steiner

Chanticleer Staff:
Editor-in-Chief: Amy K. Hughes
Managing Editor: George Scott
Senior Editor: Miriam Harris
Associate Editor: Michelle Bredeson
Assistant Editor: Elizabeth Wright
Editorial Assistants: Amy Oh, Anne O'Connor
Managing Photo Editors: Ruth Jeyaveeran, Jennifer McClanaghan
Assistant Photo Editor: Meg Kuhta
Rights and Permissions Manager: Alyssa Sachar
Photo Assistant: Stephanie Wilson
Art Director: Drew Stevens
Designers: Anthony Liptak, Vincent Mejia, Bernadette Vibar
Director of Production: Alicia Mills
Production Managers: Philip Pfeifer, Melissa Martin

Contributors:
Writer: Brian Cassie
Consultant: James Cordeiro
Icons: Vincent Mejia
Editor, Field Guide Section: Lisa Leventer

Scholastic Inc. Staff:
Editorial Director: Wendy Barish, Creative Director: David Saylor,
Managing Editor: Manuela Soares, Manufacturing Manager: Karen Fuchs

Original Series Design: Chic Simple Design

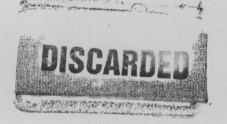